The Politics of Prevention

The Politics of Prevention

A Global Crisis in AIDS and Education

TANIA BOLER and DAVID ARCHER

Pluto Press
LONDON • ANN ARBOR, MI

JACANA

First published 2008 by Pluto Press
345 Archway Road, London N6 5AA
and 839 Greene Street, Ann Arbor, MI 48106

www.plutobooks.com

Published in South Africa 2008 by Jacana Media (Pty) Ltd
10 Orange Street, Sunnyside, Auckland Park 2092
Tel (+27 11) 628-3200

www.jacana.co.za

British Library Cataloguing in Publication Data
A catalogue record for this book is available from the British Library

ISBN   978 0 7453 2733 4   Hardback
ISBN   978 0 7453 2732 7   (Pluto Press paperback)
ISBN   978 1 77009 582 3   (Jacana paperback)

Library of Congress Cataloging in Publication Data applied for

This book is printed on paper suitable for recycling and made from fully managed and
sustained forest sources. Logging, pulping and manufacturing processes are expected
to conform to the environmental standards of the country of origin.

10   9   8   7   6   5   4   3   2   1

Designed and produced for Pluto Press by
Chase Publishing Services Ltd, Fortescue, Sidmouth, EX10 9QG, England
Typeset from disk by Stanford DTP Services, Northampton
Printed and bound in the European Union by
CPI Antony Rowe, Chippenhan and Eastbourne

Contents

Lost Summer
By Jan Gerhard Toonder, for Jeannette Boler

There has been joy, for Spring
was sweet to the frail sprig
that strove to meet life's promise:
but summer stayed away
and autumn took its place.

Your life; such brittle twig,
a plaything for the wind;
the sun without a noon,
the light of day too soon
descending into night,
the moon and stars too far,
no hiding place in sight.

We, on the beach, have watched
your being carried out
to sea and drift beyond
our clumsy human reach:
so grieve, for all that could
have been, our empty hands,
the summer lost to flight –
and wish that in the end
you found the shore where your
missed season waits,
beyond all loneliness and fright.

Acknowledgements

We would like to thank the many people who we interviewed during the course of researching this book. Some names have been changed to protect the identity of individuals who have not gone public with their status or who requested anonymity for other reasons. Extracts from interviews are set in *sans italic*. Some of the HIV material is drawn from reports written by the authors while working at ActionAid International. We would like to thank ActionAid for granting copyright to replicate this material and for their continued support during the process of writing this book. Any profits that we make, as authors, will be donated to ActionAid's education and HIV work.

Many thanks to all the individuals and organisations who shared information, commented on earlier drafts or hosted visits. These include Peter Aggleton, Flavia Antunes, Edson Arata, Jean-David Aube, Paul Bennell, Annet Biryetega, Jasmine Boler, Daopahai Buelom, Jose Carlos Veloso, Viviane Castello Branco, Dhianaraj Chetty, David Clarke, Madalena Guilhon, Tanika Gupta, Roger Ingham, Anne Jelleman, Nancy Kendall, Pornsuk Koetsawang, Christina Kon, Liliana Lauria, Gareth Lavell, Fiona Leach, Gabriella Leite, Flavio Lenz, Aadeliah Maker, Kamolpren Mana, Teopista Burungi Mayanja, Julio Mujojo, Maria Nandago, Leonard Okello, Namphung Plangraun, Rick Rowden, Amos Sibambo, Lucy Stackpool-Moore, Celia Szterenfeld, Katarina Tomasevski, Beatrice Were, Ekua Yankah and Patrick Young.

Foreword

Mary Robinson

Today's globalisation is one of stark contrasts. There are more connections – markets, people and ideas – linked than ever before. At the same time, there are more divisions – between North and South, between rich and poor, between the powerful and powerless.

Nowhere are these divides more apparent than in the twin crises in HIV and in education.

In a short period of 30 years, an epidemic of HIV has spread throughout all regions of the world, destroying the lives of millions of people. HIV has not affected all parts of the world equally. It is in poor and marginalised communities, where HIV has spread the fastest. With HIV and AIDS, groups who have already faced gross violations of their rights to live in dignity, to education and to health are being further marginalised and stigmatised. In effect, a vicious cycle is set up in which the violation of rights increases vulnerability to HIV infection which in turn leads to a further violation of rights. This explains why infection rates among young women in sub-Saharan Africa are so high.

This is why it is so urgent for people around the world to unite against an epidemic which is largely preventable. HIV is preventable through an individual's intrinsic ability to learn and change. Education is core to HIV prevention. Unfortunately, this potential has largely been underutilised and undermined by the fact that the majority of poor children in the majority of poor countries do not have the opportunity to secure their right to education.

Education is a fundamental human right in itself and a powerful enabling right – meaning that gaining an education helps people secure their other rights. It is thus an outrage that today there are over 70 million children who are not in school – the majority of whom are girls – and over 700 million adults who cannot read or write.

The Politics of Prevention brings together stories from around the world that explore and expose the nature of the twin crises – in education and in HIV. This timely book places the HIV epidemic into the context of wider international affairs. Despite huge increases in funding to tackle the HIV epidemic, HIV prevention has slipped down the international agenda and the response is hampered and weakened because of an underlying 'politics of prevention'. Little is being done to galvanise the leadership needed to support and empower marginalised and stigmatised groups.

Education can be used to bring about change on a mass scale. This book is pivotal in highlighting how individuals and communities have the power to assert their rights to education, to health and to a life in dignity.

The realisation of rights needs to serve as the foundation for responding to the globalised challenges of HIV and education. A rights-based globalised response is based on acknowledging the shared responsibilities we have for addressing global challenges and needs to affirm that our common humanity doesn't stop at national borders. We need to recognise that all individuals are equal in dignity and have the right to certain entitlements, rather than viewing them as objects of benevolence or charity. Specifically, we need to embrace the importance of gender and the need for attention to the often different impacts of HIV and education policies on women and men. Finally we need to affirm that a world which is already connected by technology and trade must also be connected by shared values, norms of behaviour and systems of accountability.

The Politics of Prevention offers us real and inspiring examples of how this vision can become a reality, advancing the notion of shared responsibility for the global challenges of HIV and education.

Mary Robinson
Former President of Ireland
Former UN High Commissioner for Human Rights
President, Realizing Rights: The Ethical Globalization Initiative

Acronyms and Abbreviations

AIDS	Acquired Immune Deficiency Syndrome
ART	antiretroviral therapy
ARV	antiretroviral
AZT	azidothymidine
DFID	UK Department for International Development
EFA	Education For All
FTI	Fast Track Initiative
GCE	Global Campaign for Education
GIPA	Greater involvement of people living with HIV and AIDS
HIV	Human immunodeficiency virus
HPV	Human papilloma virus
IMF	International Monetary Fund
NGO	Non-government organisation
OECD	Organisation for Economic Cooperation and Development
PCP	Pneumocystis carinii pneumonia
PEPFAR	President's Emergency Plan for AIDS Relief
PTR	Pupil to teacher ratio
STAR	Societies Tackling AIDS through Rights
TRIPS	Trade-related intellectual property rights
UNAIDS	Joint United Nations Programme on HIV/AIDS
UNESCO	United Nations Educational, Scientific and Cultural Organisation
UNFPA	The United Nations Population Fund
UNICEF	The United Nations Children's Fund
US	The United States of America
USAID	United States Agency for International Development
WB	World Bank
WHO	World Health Organisation
WTO	World Trade Organisation

Introduction

Early in the new millennium, the world is slowly waking up to the enormity of an epidemic that just 30 years ago was almost unknown. In 2007 alone, more than 2 million people died because of AIDS.[1] The epidemic has stealthily weaved its way through humanity, exposing divisions and creating new turmoil. It has sharpened the gulf between the few 'haves' and the majority of 'have-nots'. This epidemic has deepened the chasm between those who see religion in decline and those who cling to faith with unrivalled zeal, forcing unfashionable concepts such as morality back into public debate.

Indeed, HIV has intruded on almost every aspect of our humanity. It intrudes on the most intimate and private areas of our lives: on our sexual relations, on death, on our compassion for others and on our fears. But it can also intrude on every area of public life, impacting national economies and the basic functioning of government services.

In 2007, it was estimated that about 33 million people were living with HIV and that every day, more than 6,800 people became newly infected.[2] Although all parts of the world are affected by HIV, sub-Saharan Africa has been hardest hit, with AIDS currently the leading cause of death.[3] More than two out of three adults and nearly 90 per cent of children infected with HIV live in sub-Saharan Africa.[4]

Despite these shocking numbers, HIV prevention is possible. This book charts the role of education in preventing HIV. It draws upon interviews, case studies and evidence collected by the authors between 2003 and 2007 on behalf of ActionAid International. The stories are used to highlight real examples of how education can be used to prevent HIV and also how HIV and AIDS impact negatively on education.

As AIDS kills more and more people, we are besieged with stories of despair. But in the midst of this there are also stories of courage and hope, stories that show how we can beat the epidemic through our intrinsic ability to learn and therefore change. This book is about the power and courage of normal people: parents, teachers and children. As authors, we had the privilege to meet many courageous people who told us their stories. These individuals come from all walks of life: children with HIV and children orphaned by AIDS, teenagers and teachers, people from rich countries and poor countries, people who are highly educated and others whose right to education has been violated.

We present these stories as we found them: as a set of contrasting human stories. The child living with HIV in a village in Thailand has a story as important as that of the lobbyist challenging the IMF. The head-teacher in Uganda shares a common humanity with the sex worker in Brazil and the abstinence educator in Florida.

By telling these stories we hope to show how each individual and the choices they take in life can make a real difference, both positively and negatively, on the spread of this epidemic.

As we heard these personal stories from around the world, we saw how larger forces affect people's lives, even in the most remote places. So we also sought out people whose stories could provide an insight into these forces. We found stories of how organisations and governments have responded or failed to respond to HIV. And we discovered stories that cut right to the heart of contemporary global politics, stories that uncover disturbing new links between religion, ideology and imperialism. Through this journey we observed the enormous scale of the twin crises affecting HIV and affecting education – and we came to understand that the root causes of these crises are fundamentally political.

Chapter 1 examines the prejudice related to HIV and AIDS. Since the very first cases of AIDS were identified, the disease has been shrouded in stigma and silence. The uncertainty as to what caused AIDS and HIV created fear around the world. AIDS became the disease of gay men, sex workers or drug users before it became known as Africa's disease. Existing prejudices and stigma against these groups increased, increasing their vulnerability.

Teo's story in Chapter 1 shows us how this prejudice manifests itself on a day-to-day basis and how it feeds ignorance and denial. For both children and adults, prejudice can bring as much pain and suffering on a daily basis as the virus itself. Because of the stigma associated with HIV, people are less likely to be tested in the first place, for fear of finding out that they have HIV. It is estimated that more than 80 per cent of people with HIV do not even know they have the virus.[5] Indeed, stigma has also acted as a significant obstacle for people to access HIV services such as education, treatment and care.[6] Because of stigma, even when people learn that they have HIV, they often want to keep their status a secret.

Addressing the prejudice and stigma around HIV must therefore be a major priority. Schools should be in the frontline of any such struggle. After all, prejudice is based on ignorance and schools are supposed to be places where ignorance is overcome – where children's minds are opened up. Unfortunately, in many parts of the world, this is far from being the case as the story in **Chapter 2** shows. Somchai is a twelve-year-old in Thailand who was born with HIV. Prejudice and ignorance at school meant that he was bullied about his HIV status to the point where he could no longer face going back to school. Many more children have also had to deal with the same prejudice in school.

It is estimated that more than 15 million children worldwide have already been orphaned by AIDS.[7] Orphaned children often lack parental supervision and the role of the school in their day-to-day lives becomes increasingly important. However, orphans are less likely to go to school compared with other children. Chapter 2 situates the experiences of these children orphaned by AIDS in the wider context of the 72 million children[8] around the world who are not in school today. It explores the diverse reasons why these children are excluded and how HIV and AIDS impacts on them.

Chapter 3 examines the role of education in preventing HIV. Most people get HIV through unprotected sexual intercourse, sharing un-sterilised injection equipment (mostly injecting drug users) or during childbirth. Each of these main forms of transmission can be prevented in different ways: sexual transmission is greatly reduced by using a condom or changing sexual behaviour in order to reduce risk; clean needles will prevent drug users or medical patients from becoming infected; and transmission during child birth is greatly reduced if the mother takes antiretroviral therapy (ART).

Education is beneficial to HIV prevention in two ways. First, there is increasing evidence that simply staying at school reduces one's vulnerability to HIV infection. Staying at school strengthens girls' control, confidence and negotiating abilities to decide whether to have sex, and when they do, whether to use a condom. Girls and women can be vulnerable to HIV simply because they do not have enough power to protect themselves from infection. In order not to be infected with HIV, a woman has to have control over who she has sex with and whether or not to use a condom. The sad reality is that, in too many countries, only men have this power.

However, the power of prevention is not merely restricted to staying in school. The second way in which education is key to prevention lies in the power of schools to provide HIV and AIDS education to large numbers of teenagers and children. Schools can provide information and advice to young people who are not yet sexually active and who have not yet formed behaviours that will put them at high risk of HIV infection. It is easier to shape behaviour before it is formed than to change the behaviour of older people who are already set in their ways. For those young people who are already having sex, education on HIV prevention can provide them with the knowledge and skills that they need to reduce their risk of infection. But for schools to play this crucial role they need to be functioning effectively. Unfortunately, many education systems are in a state of crisis, particularly those in the countries that are facing the biggest challenges from HIV and AIDS. Teachers are poorly trained, underpaid and faced with overwhelmingly large class sizes. The potential power of schools to prevent HIV is seriously undermined.

Chapter 4 examines what works in preventing HIV. Too often, assumptions are made that a simple transfer of basic knowledge can protect young people from infection. But peer and societal pressures are complex and knowledge is not always enough to change behaviour. Case studies from Ghana, Mozambique and South Africa show that more elaborate approaches are needed. They illustrate the power of prevention when HIV is made into a real and personal issue. In Ghana, teachers are taught to use drama to deal with their sexuality and their own risk of HIV infection. In Mozambique, the importance of involving people living with HIV in interventions is highlighted. In South Africa, education gives way to 'edutainment' in order to reach out beyond schools. It is all too easy to be negative and fatalistic about HIV. However, the case studies presented in this chapter show that HIV prevention can work.

The role of education in responding to the AIDS crisis extends far beyond HIV prevention. **Chapter 5** highlights the important role that schools can play in providing care and support for children affected by HIV and AIDS. One harsh reality of HIV is that if one parent is infected, the other parent is more likely to be infected – leading to many children losing both parents and sometimes struggling in households without any adult supervision. For many of the children orphaned by AIDS, the most stable part of their lives will be the daily routine of being at school. Drawing from an example in Thailand, Chapter 5 tells the story of one teacher who has created an environment where children affected by HIV and AIDS can thrive. This concept of a caring and supporting school environment is analysed in relation to the concepts of child-friendly schools, inclusive education and gender-responsive schools. Ideological issues start to emerge with the contestation of child-centred learning by advocates of more teacher-centred approaches and direct instruction. The chapter concludes with an example of how important peer support is for building the confidence of HIV-positive teenagers in the United Kingdom.

Chapter 6 highlights some experiences from participatory community-based approaches to HIV prevention and shows how we need to be political if we want to stop the spread of HIV. The chapter focuses on the efforts of sex workers in Brazil who came together to educate themselves, transform their own lives and tackle the negative attitudes of society. Ultimately, HIV prevention has to take this more political and rights-driven approach in order to stop the injustices upon which HIV thrives. Chapter Six also provides examples of adult learning groups who have used education on HIV to assert their rights to treatment and other services. In cases where human rights are clearly abused, legal action has sometimes been the only recourse. The final story in Chapter 6 shows the power of using human-rights treaties and the law to stop stigma and prejudice in schools.

Chapter 7 analyses the various ideological and religious influences which have shaped the way schools teach about HIV and sex. The focus in this chapter is on the increasing influence of the American government's abstinence-only approach. Starting in Florida, where abstinence-until-marriage is promoted by evangelical churches, the chapter explores how these same approaches have been exported to Africa with devastating effects on HIV prevention.

This theme of exporting models and morality to other countries is continued in **Chapter 8** where the politics of the international responses to HIV prevention are in the spotlight. Aid for HIV prevention has been highly political but often in ways that further marginalise vulnerable groups. The way in which President Bush's PEPFAR programme uses the power of money to impose an ideology is revealed. Examples from across the world highlight how the international aid industry has failed to target those who are in real need. The role of the UN in exporting its own models is also critiqued and the reasons for its failure to provide leadership on politically sensitive issues are analysed. The chapter concludes with some reflections on how diverse neocolonial practices impact on country ownership of the HIV prevention agenda.

Chapter 9 exposes wider problems with the international architecture of aid and finance, showing how these impact on efforts towards HIV prevention. Problems with the aid industry range from aid being tied to particular goods and services to the imposition of conditions and the fundamental unpredictability of pledges and disbursements. Far too little aid money for HIV prevention reaches recipient countries and far too much is wasted. Initiatives to improve coordination of aid for education and HIV are introduced and the limitations of these examined. The focus then shifts to the IMF and the way in which macroeconomic conditions on public sector spending are undermining efforts in HIV prevention around the world. Recent breakthroughs are documented and future directions outlined.

The **Concluding Remarks** draws all these threads together and explores some fundamental parallels between the changes needed in international relations and the changes needed in human relations to achieve HIV prevention.

There is no doubt that dramatic progress has been made in treating HIV – so it should no longer be a death sentence. But fewer than one in five of the people whose lives could be saved by ARV drugs actually access them.[9] In recent years, the world seems to have woken up to some of the challenges. Funding for work on HIV and AIDS has increased dramatically.[10] But most of this goes on treatment and relatively little money is spent on prevention. So HIV continues to spread – and for every one person who succeeds in getting access to treatment, six new people are infected with the virus.[11]

The impact cannot be over-stated. Whole communities have been transformed, whole societies affected. Basic assumptions of life have been made into a mockery. The young die before the old. Those who should be fit die first.

As the world finally wakes up to the AIDS crisis, billions of dollars are now being made available. But in the process, HIV prevention has become highly political. We need to understand this '**politics of prevention**' if we are to challenge some of the disturbing developments of recent years. We need to act urgently, strategically and collectively if we are not to lose future generations to a disease that can and should be prevented.

1
The Epidemic of Prejudice

GLOBAL OVERVIEW

Since 1981, more than 25 million people have died of AIDS.[1] In 2007 alone 2.5 million people were newly infected with HIV. Although all parts of the world are affected by HIV, sub-Saharan Africa has been hardest hit, with AIDS currently the leading course of death.[2] More than two out of three adults and nearly 90 per cent of children infected with HIV live in sub-Saharan Africa.

In sub-Saharan Africa, the HIV epidemic has spread over the past 30 years from east Africa (Uganda/ Tanzania/ Kenya) to southern Africa where epidemics have exploded at astonishing rates: nearly one in five adults is thought to have HIV in Namibia, Lesotho, South Africa, Swaziland and Botswana.[3] The HIV epidemic has spread very differently between regions, with lower prevalence in west Africa,[4] as well as within countries. Often HIV prevalence rates vary widely between cities (usually higher) and rural areas.

In east and southern Africa, most of the HIV epidemics are generalised, meaning that the virus has spread into the general population.[5] Countries outside this region of sub-Saharan Africa tend to still have concentrated epidemics which means that HIV is generally confined to certain sub-populations such as injecting drug users, sex workers or men who have sex with men.[6] For example, HIV is mostly contained amongst sex workers and their clients in Senegal, Thailand, Cambodia and Côte d'Ivoire. The number of countries where this is the case is probably much higher but as these groups are often so stigmatised, it is difficult to know what the actual numbers are. This is particularly the case for gay men in many parts of the world, especially Africa where many governments prefer to believe that this group does not exist. In Eastern Europe, nearly two thirds of HIV infections were caused through injecting drug use.[7]

HIV and AIDS have changed the world for millions of people. The statistics can be so overwhelming that we can all too easily forget that each one of these people has a personal story. Yet it is in the details of individual lives that we can understand the real impact of the epidemic.

Of all the countries in sub-Saharan Africa, Uganda is the one which provides a special insight into the history and the response to the epidemic. Teo is one of the millions of Ugandans whose life has changed by HIV and AIDS.

TEO'S STORY, UGANDA

Born in 1963 in Uganda, east Africa, Teopista Burungi Mayanja – or Teo for short – was one of eight children from a modest family. Although Teo studied hard at primary school and completed her exams successfully, her family could not afford to send her to secondary school. At the time, it was possible to train as a primary school teacher without a secondary education. By the time she was 18, she was qualified as a basic-grade teacher.

In 1985, she took her first job posting in Kampala, Uganda's capital, at a large primary school with more than 2,000 students. It was then that she began to hear stories of an unknown illness:

It came from the south and people fled in terror. Neighbours warned each other in hushed tones, 'If your children are still alive, beg them to leave this place of horror.' It was killing people – young people – and fast. Stories spread from village to village, each time gaining momentum. Of one thing people were certain: somewhere, for some reason, a fury had been unleashed. The blame fell on one family in Masaka – near the border with Tanzania. They had argued with a family across the border and in revenge, evil spirits from Tanzania had been released. First, they attacked the family, sparing no one. Second, the village was destroyed. And now it was spreading across the country, hunting down those who tried to run away.

Two years later, a teacher in her school died.

She was called Lena – a beautiful young teacher, a single woman with many friends. I don't think she knew she had it. The campaign had not come out by that time. She was lean-cheeked, a beautiful girl. We just assumed she was naturally thin. But she kept falling ill. I would have to cover her lessons for her whilst she was in bed ill.

Lena's boyfriend was also a teacher at the same school and within a year, both had died. As many of the teachers had been relocated to Kampala to work at the school, they were mostly living in accommodation at the school. This contributed to the rapid spread of HIV through the school:

They were all living in accommodation in the school so they would all see each other in the evenings. They were young and they kept changing their mind and

changing partners. That first teacher died soon after leaving the school in 1987.
Within a few years, another 16 teachers in that school died.

Although Teo began to realise that it was AIDS that was killing her colleagues, she was unable to convince her family that AIDS had even intruded upon their own lives. In 1987, her sister died of an AIDS-related illness. At the funeral, Teo noticed that one of her younger sisters, Rosa, had lost a lot of weight and was looking very unhealthy.

Teo tried to talk to her mother and warn her that Rosa had AIDS. Her mother was distraught. AIDS was only for bad people. How could her own daughter suggest such a terrible thing? She shouted furiously at Teo: 'I did not expect that from you of all people. How could you say that against your sister?'

Teo asked her mother if she could take Rosa back to Kampala as they had better doctors there. This seemed to make things worse. There were tears and ranting. Her mother consulted her neighbours and became convinced that the family was cursed. It was a spell and not an illness. Teo was blamed for having too much education and creating divisions and difficulties. To Teo's despair, all the neighbours agreed and decided to send Rosa to the traditional 'witch doctor' instead.

When her mother asked her for the money, Teo was torn. She could see the trauma that she had caused her mother but she was desperately worried for her sister Rosa. Against her better judgment she finally agreed to pay for the traditional healer and she returned to Kampala alone.

Three months later the news came that Rosa had died.

Rather than convincing her mother that Teo had been right, Rosa's death led her mother deeper into the world of superstition and folklore. Once again she consulted the traditional healers. On one level Teo could see this was understandable. The traditional healers offered her mother not only an explanation but a cure. If she believed her daughters had died of AIDS, there would be neither cure nor hope. Teo's mother turned against her – effectively banishing her.

But despite all the money her mother spent on the healers and witch-doctors, just four months later a third daughter died of AIDS.

At this third funeral Teo arrived again. This time Teo herself looked pale and ill. The neighbours stared and said to one another: 'See that family; now even the educated one is bewitched.' Teo's mother saw them staring. She was ashamed and desperate. Was there no end to this curse – three daughters dead in the space of seven months and a fourth looking ill? What was going on in the spirit world? For what sins was she being punished? Surely now her daughter Teo would accept that something was wrong? If she too was ill was that not proof that education and science were no protection? That the real explanation lay in the spirit world – in the religious universe? Teo's mother pleaded with her to go and visit a traditional healer herself – to be cleansed of the angry spirit – to break the curse before it was too late. Only he would be able to do something.

Teo wouldn't listen. She refused to visit the healer and returned to Kampala. Concerned about her health she went to the hospital. After an anxious wait she was told that, rather than being sick, she was in fact pregnant. Teo rejoiced and sent the news to her mother, hoping this would reassure her. Instead her mother rushed to the local traditional healer with the news and sent back a message to Kampala. You must come back and give birth in the local river – only then will the curse be lifted. Teo refused. She stayed in Kampala and gave birth in a hospital. The baby was healthy – but the rift between mother and daughter widened.

Losing three sisters to AIDS devastated Teo and the situation with her mother was making matters worse. Back at school her colleagues continued with their whispering, 'You see that one, she is also a victim because she was going to bed with so and so, who was going with so and so.' The teachers gossiped and gossiped, without ever saying the word 'AIDS'; those individuals who were the focus of slander shrank away from the crowd. Ostracised, they started to apply for transfers – either to get away from a school where everyone was pointing a finger at them or to go to a place where no one knew them. Fleeing to a new place often didn't offer the solace they sought, for as soon as they were found out, they would be forced to move again.

Even though Teo's own family had been hard hit by AIDS, the silence which enveloped AIDS at that time in Uganda meant that she was unable to talk publicly about the disease. Teo was promoted to be head-teacher of a school with 26 teachers. As the outgoing head-teacher left, he warned her: 'Sara was a good teacher but is now very ill. She is very *ill*, she is (whispering) "infected"... I was planning to transfer her.'

Teo soon found that three of the 26 teachers in her charge had HIV. Colleagues kept suggesting that she transfer them away from the school and away from their sight. Teo wanted to broach the subject with her staff but found it simply too awkward. What if the HIV-positive teachers were angry? And how could she help anyway? What could she do? She felt powerless. One option was to register them as sick; in this way they could claim sick pay while not working. After six months they had either to retire or return to school. The twist was that there was no provision for a replacement teacher if anybody took sick leave.

Then in 1997 there was a radical change to primary schooling in Uganda that made Teo's life even more complicated. President Museveni declared that the first four children in every family would be allowed to go to school for free.[8] Most people in the world take free education for granted but in Uganda, as in many African countries, parents had been expected to make a contribution – to pay school fees. Even though the amounts were modest, millions of children, particularly girls, were being excluded from school because their parents could not afford to pay.

Museveni made the pledge as part of an election campaign and it proved immensely popular. He was swept back to power ... and children were swept into the schools. Over the coming year enrolment in schools doubled and within five years it had tripled. Although Museveni did invest more money in education by using increased revenues from debt-relief (and thus increasing education spending from 2.6 per cent to 4 per cent of GDP), the additional resources were insufficient to keep up with the increased demand.

Like most schools, Teo's school was dramatically affected. Class sizes shot up. For a time there were more than a hundred children in the first grade. Inevitably the quality of education deteriorated as children received less time from the teachers, classrooms were cramped, and there were insufficient materials or textbooks to go around. Teo doubled up classes and juggled with the teaching timetable on the assumption that things would improve once new resources came in. She sent the new enrolment figures to the government on the understanding that the school would then be allocated additional teachers. But the bureaucratic hurdles in the system meant that even when she left the school four years later she had received no new teachers.

The situation was made worse by the lack of clarity about government messages relating to free primary education. Parents started sending children to school without lunch or without scholastic materials because they thought free education meant that everything was free. Confusion also arose around the role of the teachers. The government announced that local leaders should become partners in education, resulting in many wanting to take over the role of head-teacher.

All those stresses were coming to the teachers in the classroom; a class with over one hundred students, some of whom are dozing – they have not had a meal. Some of them have nowhere to sit, so you have to walk over them. And here you are, and you also feel ill. That is the kind of stress I am talking about. Given the situation at the time, teachers did not have a voice.

Overwhelmed with the new pressures, the teachers in her school who had HIV were often too weak to work. It was erratic. Perhaps one week they would be fine and the next not. Sometimes the sick teachers would sit in the classroom but be too weak to teach. The students talked about it at break time and would then go home to tell their parents.

Teo started receiving visits from worried parents – mostly mothers. For a while she was receiving such a constant stream of angry parents that she suspected that they must have had some local meeting to discuss the situation. The mothers wanted to know why their children were not being taught properly. Why was the teacher always ill? Actually they didn't care to know why the teacher was ill – they just wanted a replacement.

Teo replied diplomatically: 'I am handling the situation'. But behind the scenes she was more anxious than ever.

*   *   *

It seems rhetorical to say that prejudice kills people – but Teo's story shows that all too often the stigma attached to HIV can be as deadly as the disease itself.

A recent review suggests that the stigma related to HIV and AIDS is more severe than that associated with other life-threatening conditions and that it often extends beyond the disease itself to anybody working with people with HIV.[9] Prejudice about HIV and AIDS thrives in Europe as much as in Africa and Asia. It affects adults, teenagers and children. Prejudice takes many forms and many guises. It can be seen in a subtle shift of body language or felt in the form of direct abuse. Inevitably those who suffer from the prejudice about HIV become the most sensitive to its manifestations and often people with HIV begin to 'self-stigmatise' as they begin to feel inferior and imagine that everybody else sees them as such.[10]

For many, HIV is linked with issues of immoral behaviour such as sex work or drug use. The stigma related to HIV is therefore often reinforced and exacerbated by the stigma which already exists for groups such as gay men, drug users, prison workers or sex workers. Molly, an Irish teenager, recalls what happened when the children in her class found out she had HIV:

The worst thing was that people assumed my parents were heroin addicts. No one seemed to think it could've been sexual transmission. For me that would have been a lot better – more sort of innocent. But no, everyone assumed my parents were heroin junkies, which made it seem like it was more their fault, more self-inflicted. As soon as it came out, I couldn't face school again. No one could do anything to make it better. There's nowhere more brutal than the school playground. Where I came from there's nothing lower than having junkies for parents.[11]

Because of the stigma and fear associated with HIV, people are reluctant to get tested. Indeed, it is estimated that more than 80 per cent of people with HIV do not know they have the virus.[12] Stigma also blocks people from accessing services, including counselling and treatment.[13] Most of all, stigma means people who do test positive often keep their status a secret.

Max, a 15-year-old boy from London, England, who was born with HIV, says:

People don't need to know unless they need to know. I don't tell anyone unless I can't avoid it. I know they would react badly because people don't have a grasp of what AIDS is. I keep it to myself because it is guaranteed that, if people knew, there would be a majority against me instead of a minority. In life there's always a minority against you and you can deal with that but you can't deal so easy with a majority. If I realise that a person is okay to understand it and take it all in, and not react as if I am someone who is going to kill them if they stand near me or talk to me, then maybe I might consider telling them but I won't unless they really need to know.

If a person has a non-communicable disease – something like cancer or Parkinson's – it is their decision as to whom they tell. On the other extreme, highly infectious diseases, such as SARS, are viewed as grave threats to society and you are legally bound to notify the authorities and may even be quarantined against your will. Disclosure of sexually transmitted infections falls into somewhat of a grey area. An individual's right to confidentiality is in conflict with what many people believe is a duty to inform. In the United States, for example, 23 states currently have HIV-transmission laws. In most cases, these laws make it a crime for HIV-positive people to have sex without first disclosing their status, regardless of whether they are practising safe sex. A review of the impact of these laws concludes that:

HIV disclosure laws, which by and large omit any reference to condom use, turn the public health response to HIV upside down by implying that reliance on disclosure is an effective strategy for reducing HIV risk.[14]

With these types of laws, HIV becomes criminalised and the focus shifts away from issues such as promoting safer sex and condoms. More than 40 countries have introduced laws which impose travel restrictions on people with HIV as part of efforts to control the spread of the virus.[15] In most of these cases, people with HIV are not allowed to apply for long-term visas. Although governments have a duty to control the spread of the epidemic, they also have a duty to respect the human rights of all people, including those with HIV. These forms of travel restrictions and laws can inadvertently create more stigma, more silence and ultimately, drive HIV even more underground. Many of these laws were created at a time when little was known about HIV and public fear was at its highest.

In order to understand the stigma that has built up around HIV and AIDS, it is helpful to look historically at how the epidemic has evolved. This was a disease that first became evident among groups of people who were already stigmatised.

Since the very beginning of HIV and AIDS, the disease has been shrouded in uncertainty and silence. Most likely around since the 1970s or even earlier, the virus spread silently, without detection. It was not until 1981 when doctors began to start noticing a sudden increase in certain rare diseases (Kaposi's sarcoma and pneumocystis carinii pneumonia (PCP)) particularly among gay men in the United States.[16]

Dr. Anthony S. Fauci of the National Institute of Allergy and Infectious Diseases recalls,

It was like living in an intensive care unit all day long. The patients were very sick, and despite the best efforts of NIH's [the National Institutes of Health] dedicated doctors and nurses, most patients eventually died. There was much to learn about the new disease and much to learn about the community hard-hit by the first wave of the epidemic, gay men.[17]

It soon became obvious though that this was not just a disease for gay men. Heterosexual partners, haemophiliacs and injecting drug users started displaying this same set of unusual symptoms.

In 1982, doctors started using the acronym AIDS: Acquired Immune Deficiency Syndrome. Nobody understood yet what was causing this new disease but they were certain that it was acquired rather than inherited; they knew that it resulted in a deficiency in the immune system; and the term syndrome was used because there were a number of different symptoms rather than one single disease.[18]

At this stage, it became clear that blood transfusions that were contaminated with this unknown virus had the potential to infect hundreds of people at a time. Large numbers of haemophiliacs were developing AIDS through blood transfusions and the media raised public alarm over 'killer blood'.[19] It was not possible to screen blood as the cause of the disease was still unknown, so controversial guidelines were introduced asking blood donors who fitted a certain profile (for example, gay men or drug users) not to donate blood.

At the same time, cases of AIDS were observed in parts of Zambia and the Congo. The World Health Organisation started a global surveillance system.[20] Then in 1984, there was a breakthrough. Two sets of scientists, in the United States and France, separately isolated the virus which was causing AIDS: HIV.[21]

HIV stands for human immunodeficiency virus and is a retrovirus that attacks part of the human immune system called CD4 T cells, by either destroying or impairing them. The virus passes from person to person through contact with certain bodily fluids such as semen, vaginal fluids and blood. HIV is also present in saliva and urine, but the concentrations are so low that it is very unlikely that somebody will get HIV in this way.

Once HIV enters the body, it starts multiplying in number (known as the viral load) simultaneously destroying CD4 cells. For several years, a person with HIV may display no symptoms whatsoever. However, at some point, their immune system begins weakening until it gets to a point when the body is so 'immune deficient' that it can no longer fight off everyday infections (known as 'opportunistic infections').

A person with immune deficiency is likely to fall prey to a number of infections that are often rare in healthy people. The unusual combinations of these rare diseases were what researchers had identified as AIDS.

As HIV was discovered after AIDS, some people have argued that the term AIDS is not really needed anymore – as it is really to do with the stage of HIV infection.[22] However, the term AIDS is still used to differentiate between those with an HIV infection and those at the most advanced stage of infection, at which point the body is severely weakened. At this stage, people will often exhibit some of the following infections: chronic diarrhoea and vomiting, thrush infections of the throat; and Kaposi's sarcoma (a previously rare disease which causes painful lesions to break out, making breathing, eating and walking difficult). It can take between 10 and 15 years for someone with HIV to develop AIDS. With treatment, this period can be delayed substantially.[23]

In the five years following the discovery of HIV, there were huge advances in the ability to detect the virus in the blood. In addition, a rudimentary form of treatment called AZT (azidothymidine) was developed which was shown to slow down the advance of HIV. At the same time, it became clear that HIV was already present in many parts of Africa and Asia, and that a disease known as 'slim disease' which had been described in Uganda since the early 1980s was actually AIDS.[24]

In the 1990s, rates of HIV exploded across many parts of Africa. In just one decade the numbers infected with HIV around the world tripled from 8 million to 25 million.[25]

The 1990s was also a decade of progress with the development of an increasingly effective treatment. This started with scientists combining two existing drugs – so-called 'combination therapy' – and evolved over the next few years to become what is now known as 'antiretroviral therapy' (ART) which combined at least three antiretroviral drugs (ARVs) to suppress the HIV virus and stop the progression of the disease.[26]

Although not a cure, ARVs were – and are – very successful in drastically reducing levels of HIV in the blood. People who had almost zero counts of CD4 (the white blood cell attacked by HIV) were brought back to full health and HIV levels became so reduced that they became undetectable.

Despite there being a treatment which worked, international patent laws rendered the drugs far too expensive for all but a small minority. In the late 1990s, HIV treatment for one person cost about $15,000 a year.[27] With millions of people around the world living on less than one dollar a day, scaling up access to treatment was not even seen as an option.

At the turn of the new millennium, the inequitable access to treatment caused increasing public outrage. HIV still meant death for people in poor countries whereas in rich countries in Europe or North America, HIV had become a chronic but manageable disease.

Outraged by this injustice, civil society groups around the world united against the patent laws arguing that public health should be prioritised over a pharmaceutical company's profits. Companies in India and elsewhere started to produce cheap 'generic' versions of ARVs. In reaction, the big pharmaceutical companies protested to the World Trade Organisation (WTO).

Public anger was so strong that at the WTO meeting in Doha in 2001, ministers stated publicly that intellectual property rights should not take precedence over public health. A new system of compulsory licensing was introduced which would allow governments to buy generic copies of drugs if the prices were too high and the disease was considered to be a health emergency. Although very few countries have used the compulsory licensing, the combination of public outrage and fear of competition have forced pharmaceutical companies to drastically reduce the price of treatment.[28]

GlaxoSmithKline Plc said on Sunday it had handed over rights to its market-leading AIDS medicines in South Africa to a local generic drug firm, in an attempt to defuse a continuing row over access to treatment … Drug companies, under fire for not doing more to help poor countries, are trying to perform a balancing act by cutting prices in Africa while not jeopardising their profitable premium markets in North America and Europe.[29]

Pharmaceutical companies have now dropped the price of anti-retroviral treatment dramatically. Now, rather than costing $15,000 a year, the price is more like $150.[30]

Despite the fact that treatment is now more affordable and funding for treatment has increased, in 2007, the WHO estimated that only two out of seven people in need of treatment in poor countries were receiving it.[31] The consequence is that more than 2 million people died from AIDS in 2007.[32] Many of these deaths could have been prevented.

*   *   *

It is estimated that HIV has now affected over 80 per cent of Ugandan families;[33] so Teo is not alone. After losing three sisters in 1987 she continues to be personally affected. In 2003 another sister died of AIDS. And to this day, she helps a fifth sister, paying $25 for her anti-retroviral treatment every month. Thankfully, she is now reconciled with her mother. After seeing other relatives and friends die of AIDS, and having been exposed to government awareness campaigns in the

1990s, Teo's mother has finally accepted that it was indeed AIDS that killed her daughters and is able to talk about it. Teo is now heading one of Uganda's teacher unions and campaigning for increased access to treatment for teachers as well as all those in need.

Teo's story shows the devastating power of prejudice. For both children and adults, prejudice can bring as much pain and suffering on a daily basis as the virus itself. Addressing the prejudice and stigma and silence around HIV must therefore be a major priority.

2
The Impact of AIDS on Education

Like a pebble dropped in a pool, HIV sends ripples to the edges of society, affecting first the family, then the community, then the nation as a whole.

UNAIDS, 2007[1]

In countries where HIV has spread into the general population, the impact of HIV and AIDS has been significant, often not confining itself to the individuals but beginning to affect great swathes of society.[2] Each person is embedded in a network of family, peers, communities and society. As a person becomes ill and dies, there are important consequences for his or her family – particularly for any dependants such as children or the elderly.

When enough individuals become infected with HIV, the consequences begin to have an impact on whole communities, affecting local livelihoods, social life and cultural norms. The next stage, in very seriously affected countries, is that whole societies begin to feel the consequences of unprecedented levels of mortality.[3] HIV ceases to be just a public-health issue and potentially becomes a societal issue which can impact nationally on the economy and on the provision of all services, including education.

Politically, the potentially devastating impact of HIV epidemics around the world has been used to mobilise resources and action. The international donor community has been lobbying African governments, arguing that the very institutions holding society together are under threat: health systems, education systems and industries.[4]

Because HIV is mostly transmitted through unprotected sexual intercourse, the virus has spread most rapidly through adults who are in the most productive part of the human life cycle (both in terms of procreation and economically). In highly prevalent countries, there is a huge impact from having these adults falling sick and dying. The two most obvious consequences are the economic impact and the unprecedented number of children who become orphaned by AIDS.

When a family becomes affected by HIV or AIDS, there are multiple economic consequences. First, there are the increased costs for medicines and then the fact that the sick person may be too ill to work, so there is a loss in income. As the person's health deteriorates further, other family members will need to care for the sick family member. In many circumstances, this often includes children staying at home to look after sick parents, especially if one parent has already died. These children might have to skip school or if they are older will have to stop working, meaning that a second source of income is lost. The research from highly prevalent countries in east and southern Africa shows overwhelmingly that households affected by HIV and AIDS become poorer and poorer.[5]

The impact of AIDS is often felt as an immediate and severe shock (short-term impact); but there are also more complex, gradual and long-term changes (long-term impact).[6] For instance, when a parent dies, a child might have to move house – a sharp and readily observable consequence. A few years later, that child might drop out of school because of emotional stress and poverty – both indirectly triggered by the death of their parent.

Both HIV-positive children and children orphaned by AIDS suffer from HIV-related stigma, at home and at school. In some countries, children with HIV or orphans have been denied their right to education because of ignorance and discrimination. Somchai was one of those children.

SOMCHAI'S STORY, THAILAND

In Thailand, government primary schools have to accept all children equally, regardless of their status or background. But having the right to go to school is not always enough – especially if the school environment is unwelcoming.

Somchai was just seven years old when he came home from school in a torrent of tears. It took his mother several anxious hours to find out what had happened. Had he been bullied? Had he failed some exam? Somchai's silence finally broke. Holding back his tears, he told his mother that all the children had ganged up on him, taunting him; 'Your father died of AIDS', they had shouted. None of the children knew what AIDS was – but they knew it was bad. They had surrounded him, pointing at the skin infections that ravaged his face and chanting 'You must be infected too ... you're diseased'.

It is a scene that resonates in school playgrounds around the world. Somchai felt humiliated, dirty, unwanted. In her efforts to console him, his mother lied. 'No, this is not true. You just get sick. You don't have AIDS', even though she knew that Somchai had been born with the virus. She persuaded him to go back to school the next day and the day after – but every day was a struggle. He would come back home crying and sit sullenly in the corner. When he did talk it was to complain that none of the children ever played with him. Partly he blamed himself – because of his weak lungs he rarely had the energy to run around. But in the past there had always been someone to sit with him and talk. Now he was shunned; left alone. No one would come up to him unless it was to abuse or mock him.

Finally it was too much. Somchai pleaded with his mother to let him stay at home – to teach him to read herself. His mother was worried, feeling unqualified for the task. For her, education was everything. She was aware that she had never had sufficient chances herself. She wanted a different, better life for her children. But she could not bear to think of the daily torture Somchai was enduring, so she agreed – and she did what she could to teach him to read and write.

It was normal practice in their village that a teacher would visit within a few days of an unexplained absence. But this time, even when the teacher did come by the house on some other, unrelated business, not a word was spoken about Somchai. The school seemed happy to forget him.

Somchai has not been to school since. His mother tried to help at first but then her own health deteriorated. Four months later she died, leaving Somchai orphaned at the age of 11. 'I don't remember going to school', he confesses. 'I don't study at home. There is nobody to teach me now. My mother used to teach me to write a little … but I cannot read.'

After his mother died, Somchai went to live with his aunt. She was too scared to send him back to school again:

One part of me wants him to go to school but on the other hand if getting education means getting that treatment then I don't want him to go. I worry that it would be the same in another school. The neighbours stay away from Somchai. There is one boy who likes to play with him but his parents don't like it so he comes here in secret. The villagers talk to us but not to him. Even today Somchai still does not know he has AIDS – he never asks why he gets sick, he just complains that it hurts.

Somchai's family is supported by a local NGO called AIDS Access. Namphung Plangraun is the regional coordinator and has helped the family get treatment for Somchai. Without treatment, about 50 per cent of HIV-positive babies will die before their second birthday, with the vast majority dying by the age of ten.[7] With treatment, the chances of a mother passing on HIV to her baby during childbirth decrease to less than 2 per cent and children on treatment can now expect to grow up into healthy adults.[8]

Despite the dramatic differences that antiretroviral treatment can make to a person's life, UNICEF currently estimates that less than 10 per cent of HIV-positive pregnant women receive drug therapies to prevent the transmission of HIV to their infants and less than 10 per cent of HIV-positive children in need of treatment are receiving it. Given the low numbers of pregnant women accessing services to prevent mother-to-child transmission (PMCT), the number of babies being born with HIV is increasing rapidly. In 2007, this number increased from 1.5 million to 2.5 million globally with nearly 90 per cent living in sub-Saharan Africa.[9]

Thailand is one of the strongest success stories in terms of controlling HIV rates. The number of new infections has been decreasing year by year[10] and very early on in the epidemic, the previous government took the bold decision to work closely with sex workers (launching a 100 per cent condom programme) as well as to provide treatment to a large number of children and adults.[11] Babies of HIV-positive women are regularly tested for HIV and UNICEF estimates that more than 95 per cent of HIV-positive children in need of treatment are accessing it.[12]

Somchai is now on treatment but he is still not at school and still not aware of his HIV status. Namphung is anxious that after all this time, after the death of both his father and mother, Somchai has still not been told that he was born with HIV. It is not her job to tell him and yet in this case the truth could have a dramatic impact. It could help him understand that his health problems over the years are not a mystery but rather are linked – and that with the new antiretroviral therapy his prospects have been transformed.

This is a common problem. More than half of the 116 children Namphung works with across Chiang Rai have never been told of their status – and yet, like Somchai, most would surely have their own deep but unspoken suspicions.

Not having his status confirmed has not reduced the stigma faced by Somchai and has not helped him get on with an ordinary life. Namphung argues that young children, for example under seven years old, are best off not knowing (as they would struggle to understand and might let other children know inappropriately – which often leads to negative consequences). However, children like Somchai, over ten years old, have a right to know their status. They would be able to understand and the information would help them to make sense of many things.

Somchai is not the only child who has been locked away by their own family because of their HIV status. The intentions are often a bizarre concoction; part love and a desire to protect the child, part shame and a desire to hide the child. In a few reported cases children have been rejected outright by their parents and thrown out of the family home.[13] But much more common is the subtle rejection, the progressive isolation of the child.

In this situation, education plays a critical role: schools can help bring children out again, making them feel included. Yet school is all too often the last thing on the minds of the parents or guardians of children like Somchai. Most people see schooling as a type of investment for the future. Children go through school in order to be able to get a better job, a better position in society. What is the point of such a long-term investment for children who are likely to die? Why look to the future of a child who you believe has no future?

Without access to treatment, children with HIV were often seen as children without a future. Although not right, some families have chosen to make their HIV-positive child's short life as easy as possible, keeping them at home all day where they can be loved, cared for, protected. But gradually that protection becomes the biggest obstacle.

Sending a child to school is often not seen as being of immediate value in itself, here and now. The focus is on the outputs, the completion of grades and success in exams which offer a passport to a better future.[14] Yet, for a child like Somchai, the most crucial part of going to school would be the experience of being there – day to day. Of course it could be a terrible experience if children discriminate and bully as they did before. But if the school focuses on creating a safe and creative environment then the experience would transform Somchai's life. It would not just transform his future prospects but also transform his daily life experience, how he relates to others, how he feels about himself, and increase his own sense of value and purpose.

Not only has HIV meant that children like Somchai do not want to go to school but it has also meant that thousands more orphans and children affected by HIV have dropped out of school, often because they are caring for sick parents or because they can no longer afford school.[15]

THE ORPHAN CRISIS

Children can be affected by HIV in multiple ways such as through the death of a parent, parental illness, living in a household which has taken in an AIDS orphan, or HIV-related stigma and discrimination.[16] However, the most visible impact of AIDS on children is the exploding number of orphans. Given that so many people are dying of AIDS, it is predicted that by 2010, 18 million children will have lost a parent because of the disease.[17]

The crisis is worst in sub-Saharan Africa where there are an estimated 11.4 million children orphaned by AIDS.[18] The family structure in many parts of Africa is very different from the one in Europe. Households are typically much larger and consist of an extended family with different generations living together.[19] If a parent dies, it is normally common practice for the extended family to take on the responsibility of looking after orphaned children.[20] Stories of ten or twenty orphans living with their grandparents are not uncommon.

Given the unprecedented rise in the number of orphans, it appears that these coping systems are becoming over-stretched and in many places, traditional extended family systems simply cannot cope.[21] In these cases, children sometimes end up living by themselves with no adult supervision – creating 'child-headed households'. In other cases, children might be sent to an institution and some will end up living on the street.

Although children are often orphaned for reasons other than AIDS, the syndrome stands out because of the increased likelihood that if one parent is HIV-positive the other parent will also be infected with HIV. Therefore children affected by AIDS face a substantial risk that both parents might die within a relatively short period of time.[22] Without AIDS, UNICEF predicted that the total number of dual orphans (children who have lost both parents) in sub-Saharan Africa would decrease between 1990 and 2010. Instead, because of AIDS, the total number of dual orphans is predicted to triple by 2010.[23]

With the massive increase in the number of orphans in Africa, schools have been struggling to deal with the new challenges which are inherent when a substantial proportion of a class experiences their parents becoming ill and dying. Although the reasons why are not fully understood, increasing evidence shows that these orphaned children are dropping out of school at much faster rates than their peers.[24] One reason is certainly poverty. As parents become ill and die, resources available for education decrease and hence orphans are more likely to drop out of school than other children, as school fees and other education costs become unaffordable. Older children who would normally be in school are dropping out in order to find employment and compensate for the loss in earnings from the ill or dead parent.[25] However, poverty does not explain the entire educational disadvantage which is experienced by orphans. It is increasingly clear that there can be psychosocial damage which leads orphans to drop out of school. Longitudinal research in KwaZulu-Natal, South Africa, showed that when fathers die, both girls and boys do worse at school. Although poverty only explained part of this disadvantage, the main cause of dropping out for girl orphans was pregnancy.[26]

In order to fully understand why orphans and children affected by HIV are more likely to drop out of school, it is important to understand the wider issue of poverty, vulnerable children and education.

CHILDREN OUT OF SCHOOL NUMBER 72 MILLION

HIV and AIDS have impacted on the education of millions of children such as Somchai, but the level and nature of this impact has been made even more severe by the already existing crisis in education in many parts of the world. Globally there are more than 72 million children who are not in school. It is difficult to grasp the magnitude of this figure. This is more than all the children in developed countries who *are* going to school.[27] What outrage would there be if every child in Western Europe and North America was not in school? Almost half of these 72 million children who don't go to school live in sub-Saharan Africa – the region where HIV and AIDS are having the most serious impact.[28]

Education is a fundamental human right, embedded in numerous international conventions and treaties, as well as regional charters. Indeed, almost all national constitutions guarantee the right to basic education. Yet this right is denied to tens of millions of children.

Despite the size of the figure of out-of-school children there are many people who are celebrating the remarkable progress that has been made in recent years. In 2000, there were 100 million children who were not in school – and to reduce this figure by 25 million in the context of population growth has meant that in real terms more than 45 million more children are in school today than were in 2000.

This is progress, but nowhere near the progress that has been promised on repeated occasions by governments around the world. In 1990, governments signed up to achieving education for all by 2000. They failed. So they repeated the promise, deferring the deadline to 2015. But on current projections many countries will fail to hit this new target and some are not expected to get all children into school until the next century.[29]

The children who are not in school today are not a random collection. In general they are not children in rich Western economies – though some children in these countries do struggle to access and stay in school. Rather they are children in Africa, Asia and Latin America. But neither are they just any children in these countries. Perhaps predictably, it is the poor children who are not in school.[30] But of course it is not all poor children. Many children from poor backgrounds get some form of education. Those who are unlikely to do even this fall into clear categories. These categories overlap; a child who falls under multiple categories and is poor and orphaned is at even more risk of dropping out of school.

The first category, and the largest, is girls. In many countries, a girl from a poor household is much less likely to go to school than her male peers. This is most acute in south and west Asia where over two thirds of the 16 million children out of school are girls.[31] A significant divide is notable also in many sub-Saharan African countries.

There are many reasons for this disparity, but the overriding explanation is patriarchy. In some societies, girls are not valued as much as boys. Often the blame is placed on 'cultural attitudes' – but these attitudes are so widespread that it seems wrong to suggest that it is tied to a locally defined set of traditional beliefs. In many communities around the world parents do not see the education of girls as a good investment. The Global Campaign for Education conducted a study into why girls are less likely to go to school and found that parents had a host of reasons[32] such as not wanting to invest in girls' education because girls would only become housewives and leave the parental home; girls were needed at home to cook and care for siblings. Parents also expressed concern that girls might be attacked on the way to school and that it was safer for them to stay at home. The reasons are multiple – but the impact is clear and widespread.

Being a girl can be a disadvantage and this disadvantage is amplified if the girl lives in a poor rural area. Geographical location is a major determinant of educational opportunities; the more remote the community, the lower the opportunities. Many national statistics provide data nationally or by district, failing to capture the distinction between urban and rural areas even within districts. One exception is a study that looked closely at 20 countries, finding that while 88 per cent of urban boys in those countries went to school, only 79 per cent of rural girls had the same chance.[33] In some countries the differences were even more startling. In Niger, just 45 per cent of boys living in towns go to school – but girls in rural areas do dramatically worse, with just 15 per cent of them enrolling in primary school. The sheer distance from the home to the 'local' school can be a massive obstacle. In some respects, the miracle is that millions of children do overcome this, walking for an hour or even two hours each way every day.

Children from any minority community, such as an indigenous community, an ethnic or linguistic minority, or a low-caste group, are less likely to go to school.[34]

Orphans are one of the clearest categories of children out of school around the world, either because they are forced into early adulthood, becoming heads of households themselves, or because they go to live with another family where they might be disadvantaged compared with other children in the household.[35] This, of course, is a category where AIDS has been a strong shaping factor, but it is not the only factor.

In urban areas, the children of parents living in illegal slums, street children or children whose parents are drug addicts face particular challenges.[36] Indeed, these groups can be those most vulnerable to HIV whether through sharing needles as injecting drug users or engaging in sex work to survive. Children from urban areas are also more likely to be living in contexts of higher HIV prevalence.[37]

Another clear category of children excluded from school is that of those who are affected by conflict. Indeed, over 40 per cent of children who are not in school today live in conflict-affected or fragile states. These children may be internally displaced or refugees, their schools or teachers may have been targeted in conflict, or the basic functioning of the state may simply have collapsed, making the provision of schooling impossible.[38] Conflict situations are also associated with an increased spread of HIV, whether through the use of rape or violence or through displacement and the consequent disruption of social norms for large numbers of people.[39]

There is one further category which cuts across all the others: disability. If a child is disabled and poor, then educational opportunities are severely diminished. One estimate suggests that more than one third of out-of-school children in the world have a disability and that less than 10 per cent of disabled children in Africa are in school.[40] Where they exist, traditional community support systems for disabled children are often undermined or overwhelmed by the spread of HIV and AIDS, making it even less likely that disabled children will have access to school. This already marginalised minority is pushed even further down the list of government priorities.[41]

So what do all of these children who are not in school do? In most cases they are working.[42] They may be working in the fields, in their homes, or for other people. Indeed, with very few exceptions (such as the disabled) it is fair to say that any child not in school is a child-labourer. They contribute to the household economy. This is often used as a justification: such children should not be expected to go to school because their families depend on them for desperately needed income. But this simply perpetuates a cycle of poverty. The MV Foundation in India[43] has shown that systematic campaigning to eliminate child labour actively benefits the poorest households, enabling poor parents to find better-paid work which was previously taken by children while their children can go to school and invest in the future.

There is, however, no doubt that almost all the above categories of children are united by poverty. And in the absence of systematic campaigns to eliminate child labour, individual families do find themselves depending on their children to contribute to household income. In this context, sending a child to school has an indirect cost in terms of lost income. The problems really multiply when there is also a direct cost – such as school fees – to bear.

It is a shocking fact that children have to pay to go to primary school in 92 countries around the world.[44] Ironically it is children who live in the poorest countries who are most likely to have to pay. In past decades, aid agencies such as the World Bank supported a policy of cost-sharing across Africa, in which it was assumed that governments could not afford to educate all their children unless parents shared the cost.[45] This meant that parents had to pay a 'user fee' to send their children to the local primary school. The result was that many parents could not afford to educate their children, or that parents had to choose which of their children to send to school. More often than not it was the girls they kept behind – because the education of boys was seen as a better investment.[46] Sons may use their education to earn more to support the family in future, while daughters have fewer prospects for paying back the investment, especially in cultures where they are destined to move in with their husband's family on marriage.[47]

In recent years there have been massive campaigns to abolish these user fees. Prominent amongst the global activists calling for this abolition was the Global AIDS Alliance.[48] This organisation recognised that when children had to pay to go to school, AIDS orphans and children affected by HIV were among the first to suffer. Indeed, the worst impacts of HIV and AIDS are felt by the categories of children above – where HIV or AIDS adds another layer to the discrimination and marginalisation from which they already suffer.

These campaigns to abolish fees have had some great successes. In just three countries, Uganda, Tanzania and Kenya, more than 8 million children enrolled in school after fees were abolished. Countries that have abolished fees have also seen gender gaps diminishing rapidly, proving that girls were being held back from enrolling by the direct costs of schooling.[49]

The AIDS epidemic has thrown up new and difficult challenges for the education community. In many cases, children who are already being denied their right to education are amongst those most vulnerable to HIV infection as they grow up.[50] Girls are more vulnerable than boys. Any child struggling for economic survival is at great risk from sexual exploitation. Children whose communities have been devastated by war live in a context where HIV can spread more rapidly. It is a dreadful irony that it is the children who are already denied their right to education that are potentially those who have the most to gain. Education, as the next chapter shows, has the power to help protect them from HIV. But for many, this remains an impossible dream.

When these vulnerable children are directly affected or infected by HIV their vulnerability is further amplified. They are even less likely to be able to afford to go to school because AIDS will have exacerbated their poverty.[51] If they do go to school, the evidence suggests that many suffer psychosocial problems or lack a supportive home environment to help them make the most of the opportunity.[52] They are more likely to attend school irregularly or to drop out completely. And, as Somchai's story illustrates, they are more likely to suffer from extreme stigma and discrimination – because many are already stigmatised or discriminated against for other reasons. Bullies often pick most viciously on those who are already perceived as being weak or different.[53]

If children like Somchai are fortunate enough to have access to ARV treatment, many may be unable to follow through the treatment effectively, whether owing to low literacy, poor nutrition or unsettled daily routines. HIV is a multiplier, feeding on the existing vulnerabilities of children. Education is one of the best hopes for these children – but to respond effectively we need first to address the existing inequalities in education systems which are already failing so many children.

3
A Crisis in Education

Societies entrust schools with the enormous responsibility for preparing children for their journey through the world. Today that means preparing them to navigate their way in a world with HIV. Each new year-group in a school offers a new opportunity for preventing HIV – they could be the first HIV-free generation. As such, each year that children leave school without the knowledge, attitudes and behaviour that could protect them from HIV is a huge missed opportunity.

In the midst of the despair and havoc that HIV causes, education stands out as a beacon of hope. Simply staying longer at school means that young people are in a better position to protect themselves from HIV.

One of the latest trends observed in Africa is the increasing feminisation of the pandemic. Almost three-quarters of the young people living with HIV in Africa are female[1] and overall almost 61 per cent of adults living with HIV in 2007 were women.[2] Despite this alarming trend, women know less than men about how HIV is transmitted and how to prevent infection.[3]

Can education really make a difference for these girls and young women? In the past, the evidence seems to have been unclear. There were some people who argued that more-educated people were more vulnerable to HIV infection because education brings mobility and money, both of which mean more sexual opportunities and more risks.

In 2006, ActionAid undertook a systematic review of the evidence of the relationship between education and vulnerability to HIV.[4] The research showed that before 1995, educated girls were indeed more vulnerable to HIV, as levels of awareness were low. But since 1995, as sex education has improved and a greater understanding of HIV prevention has developed, more-educated girls are less likely to contract HIV. Today, secondary education provides African girls with the power to make sexual choices that prevent HIV infection. Girls who are educated are more likely to wait before having sex, are much more likely to use condoms when they do have sex, and are therefore at much less risk of contracting HIV. Indeed, girls who complete secondary school are up to five times less likely to contract HIV than girls with no education – and are between four and seven times more likely to use a condom, as Figure 1 shows.

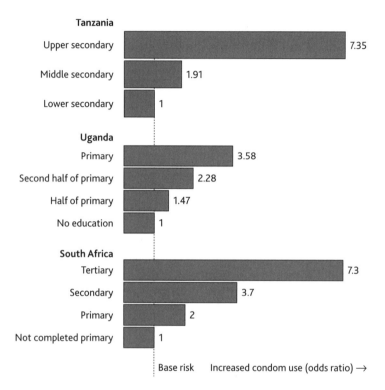

Figure 1   Condom use by level of education

The findings of this report, entitled *Girl Power*, challenged the increasingly vocal lobby that claimed it was inappropriate to promote condoms widely in the fight against HIV because an increasing number of young people is using them. It revealed that schools and teachers are the most trusted source for young people to learn about HIV, and that school attendance ensures greater understanding of prevention messages.

Why does staying in school reduce young people's vulnerability to HIV infection? The research highlighted several possible reasons, shown in Table 1.

Table 1   Potential pathways through which education might affect girls' risk of HIV infection

	Attendance at school	Higher educational attainment
Increased risk of HIV	Potential gender discrimination or sexual abuse by older boys or teachers	Greater confidence to suggest safe sex practices such as condom use
Decreased risk of HIV	Smaller sexual networks with young people of similar age who negotiate positive attitudes towards protective behaviours	Greater confidence to suggest safe sex practices such as condom use
	Higher levels of direct contact with HIV-prevention education	Greater capacity to negotiate safe sexual practice with partners
		A positive outlook for the future provides an incentive to avoid HIV infection
		Higher socioeconomic status leads to greater likelihood of STIs being treated or more capacity to buy condoms

The positive impacts of education include evidence that education strengthens girls' control, confidence and abilities to negotiate whether to have sex, and when they do, whether to use a condom. Girls and women are vulnerable to HIV simply because they do not have enough power to protect themselves from infection. In order not to be infected with HIV, a woman has to have control over who she has sex with, as well as when and how she has sex. The sad reality is that, in too many countries, only men have this power. For this reason alone, HIV prevention messages continue to be unsuccessful as they fail to tackle women's sense of sexual powerlessness.

There is also good evidence that peer-group solidarity within school strengthens girls' social networks and creates more responsible attitudes to sexual behaviour, safer sex and HIV. In contrast, girls who drop out of school are more likely to enter into adult sexual networks, where older partners with more experience and power dictate the 'rules' of sexual engagement.

The level of a young woman's education relative to her male partner's level of education also has important consequences. In many African settings, it remains socially acceptable for men to have many sexual partners, but unacceptable for women to do so.[5] Within these same settings, women are often more likely to leave school early, be unemployed or earn low wages.[6] These women are therefore entering into sexual relationships characterised by a significant power imbalance.

Such power imbalances within relationships are compounded by the common practice of young women going out with much older men. Older men might be seen as better options as boyfriends and husbands because they are in a better position to provide material support. Gifts and money are seen by many as an intrinsic component of any sexual relationship,[7] thus further increasing women's economic dependence.

Both the inferiority in age and the economic dependence of women decreases their power to negotiate within sexual relationships. What implications does this power imbalance within relationships have for HIV vulnerability? The problem is that it is often the men who dictate when to have sex and how. Since many men prefer not to use condoms,[8] their wishes – within an unequal relationship – are very likely to prevail.

Sexual violence is an extreme manifestation of this power imbalance within relationships and may particularly affect women who have not received much education, and who in turn are less able to negotiate within a relationship. Each of the scenarios above suggests that education is a positive factor in reducing HIV vulnerability for young women – but this is not always the case. Power imbalances within relationships are never more obvious than in relationships between a teacher and a student. Although the evidence is currently mostly anecdotal or qualitative in nature, an increasing number of studies suggest that some male teachers in African schools abuse their position of power to initiate sex with female students.[9] For the economic and power-related reasons cited above, it may be the case that some female students and their parents encourage such relationships. Whatever the circumstances, the gross power imbalance between a teacher and a student can place a young woman in a position of high vulnerability.[10]

Challenging sexual violence directly is not easy precisely because this is an extreme feature of a deeper culture of violence towards girls and women. There is a continuum which is rooted in the strict demarcation of gender roles, which bring girls multiple workloads from an early age. This feeds discrimination which creates an environment for harassment, within which sexual abuse or violence becomes almost tolerated.

Schools are supposed to be places that offer a safe environment for children. They should offer spaces where prejudice and discrimination are challenged and values of tolerance and equality are celebrated. But this is not always the case. Girls often face violence on the way to school, in the school grounds and even in the classroom.[11]

Research conducted across twelve countries,[12] including countries as diverse as Ethiopia, Ghana, Mozambique, Afghanistan and Vietnam, showed that violence faced in and around schools was a significant factor in forcing girls out of the education system. The study showed that girls potentially faced sexual harassment in the school environment from education staff, teachers and male students. Corporal punishment and public shaming by school authorities and teachers perpetuated a culture of violence that led to absenteeism and low self-esteem among girls. From across the countries studied, many parents feared that their daughters would be raped or abducted on their way to or from school – and this gave them a rationale for keeping girls at home.

In response to an increasing awareness of the violence which girls are subjected to, a wide range of actors is coming together, from ministries of education, teacher unions, NGOs and foundations to challenge all forms of violence against girls in and around schools. Across east and southern Africa a 'Model Policy' was developed in 2006[13] which seeks to bring together policy and legislation to prevent violence against girls in and around schools and protect victims, ensuring that confidential reporting can lead to effective action against perpetrators of abuse. This has now been approved and extended by key actors across west Africa.[14]

Certainly action is needed as girls need to be able to enrol and stay in school. Where violence in any form prevents this, it needs to be addressed head-on, even where this means challenging cultural norms.

Although violence in schools can in some contexts increase girls' vulnerability to HIV infection, it seems clear from the *Girl Power* report that, overall, schools do offer protection against HIV. Simply staying longer in school will reduce young people's chances of getting HIV. However, the power of prevention is not merely restricted to staying in school. This is just one element. After all, although people who have been to school might be less likely to get HIV, there are still far too many educated people becoming infected every day.

Another element is the ability of schools to provide HIV and AIDS education to large numbers of teenagers and children. Schools can provide information and advice to young people who are not yet sexually active – who have not yet formed behaviours that will put them at high risk of HIV infection. It is easier to shape behaviour before it is formed than to change the behaviour of older people who are already set in their ways.

Recognising the potential of schools to deliver HIV and AIDS education, donors have invested huge financial and human resources in trying to teach about HIV and AIDS in schools. However, teaching about HIV in schools is hampered by a wider crisis in education.

THE SOUND OF SILENCE

In 2002, we set up a research project in western Kenya (Nyanza province) and southern India (Tamil Nadu) to investigate how schools had responded to the new curriculum on HIV and AIDS. The research teams interviewed more than 4,000 teachers, students and parents in 60 randomly selected schools. The findings are summarised in ActionAid's report *The Sound of Silence*.[15]

First, we investigated the level of demand for AIDS education. Some teachers expressed concern that the parents opposed HIV education:

Teachers should not earn a bad name from the parents. When a teacher teaches HIV/AIDS, there is a slight restlessness in class. The students go home and tell this to their parents who say that the teacher is obscene.

Then parents come to school to question the teacher as to why the teacher has been teaching dirty things in class to students. We cannot keep explaining to the parent that it is part of the syllabus.

Female teacher, India

However, over 85 per cent of parents interviewed supported schools to teach about HIV. It was really just a minority – but a vocal minority – which opposed the curriculum.

Most of the parents feel embarrassed to discuss AIDS with their children so they like us learning about it at school.

Girl student, Kenya

In both countries, but particularly India, parents did not often talk to their children about sex and HIV so actually welcomed the school taking on this responsibility (see Figure 2).

In terms of actually teaching about HIV, the research found that teachers faced significant barriers in communication. Teachers were selectively teaching the AIDS curriculum by either not teaching the

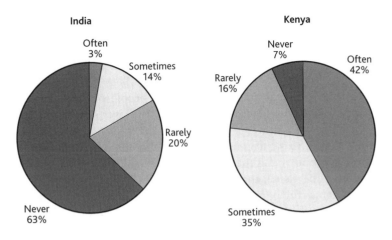

Figure 2   The frequency with which parents talk to their children about HIV and sex

lessons at all (in both India and Kenya); teaching about HIV but avoiding any discussion of sex (common in India); or teaching about HIV prevention only in terms of sexual abstinence.

It was clear that in some circumstances, teaching HIV awareness put teachers in a difficult position. For many of them, keeping silent on certain aspects of the curriculum was the easiest solution. Teachers had their own views on acceptable and unacceptable sexual behaviour, which were not always in line with certain parts of the curriculum. For example, some of the curriculum promoted condoms as a way to prevent HIV, but some of the teachers themselves were against condoms.

The challenge is to train teachers to avoid confusing their own personal views with scientific facts about condoms, and to emphasise the importance of scientifically accurate information. In the light of the many scientifically inaccurate statements about condoms that emerge from the Vatican and the United States, this task is not an easy one. This is especially true in Kenya, where prominent leaders are strongly opposed to condoms. In fact, many teachers saw the position of religious institutions on HIV as a barrier:

The religious leaders oppose AIDS education, giving culture as an excuse. Actually, we teach AIDS education in order to protect our culture only. We have to accept the changing world and accept the changing needs too.

Head-teacher, India

Being a Catholic-sponsored school, the use of condoms is definitely disapproved of and abstinence is taught to the girls. There is a motto of 'close your thighs and open your books'.

Head-teacher, Kenya

In order to discuss condoms with young people, one must assume that young people might be having sex. However, the underlying societal assumption is that young people are not having and should not have sex. This makes talking about condoms almost impossible, as adults cannot admit that young people might be having sex in the first place. If a teacher challenges or breaks this taboo the teacher risks being seen as the person responsible for corrupting children rather than protecting them. This wider denial of adolescent sexuality makes it awkward for teachers to talk about HIV and sex in school.

Most of the problems faced by teachers in teaching about HIV in India and Kenya were related to wider problems in the national education systems of the two countries. It was almost impossible for schools to take on the additional burden of teaching about HIV when that wider education system was in crisis. The research also showed that there was a wholly inadequate level of training and in-service support available for teachers on any subject, let alone HIV and AIDS. There was a shortage of basic teaching materials. Textbooks were a rarity.

In both countries teachers spoke of an overloaded curriculum that was already too much for any teacher to deliver. How could a whole new issue be introduced without any time being allocated? Ministries of education have an incredible capacity to add new priorities and new responsibilities for teachers – without ever taking anything away.

We do not have enough time to teach about HIV/AIDS, as we are already burdened with enough workload. We are always in a rush to complete the syllabus.

Teacher, India

THE POVERTY OF SCHOOLING

India and Kenya are not untypical. The financial crisis in education, explored in more detail in Chapter 9, means that many governments across Africa, Asia and Latin America are struggling to find funding for anything more than teachers' salaries. The existing wage bill often takes up more than 90 per cent of the education budget – and little is left over for other investments.[16] One area that has suffered is teacher training. Despite a rising demand for more teachers as school enrolment rises, many teacher-training colleges in Africa have been closed and many others are run down. Colleges that once attracted the best graduates and inducted them into a highly valued profession are now demoralised institutions with decaying infrastructure. The status of the profession has diminished. Pre-service teacher training courses that once ran for three years have been cut to two years or just one year. For example, in Mozambique, students who have just completed the tenth grade of their schooling can now qualify as teachers by taking a one-year training course.[17]

The World Bank has played a confusing role in this, suggesting on the one hand that governments should invest in education but on the other hand that there is little point in investing in teacher training. At a recent meeting of African ministers of education, a senior World Bank official argued that it was a waste of resources to invest in pre-service teacher training (training to become qualified as a teacher) and that anyone can teach.[18] It is no surprise then that the World Bank has actively promoted the introduction of non-professional teachers in many countries, particularly in west Africa – in other words, students who have completed secondary schooling, or sometimes just lower secondary, are recruited as teachers in primary schools without being given any training at all. The term 'non-professional' for this group is rightly applied by Education International, the international federation of teacher unions, that argues that unqualified teachers deprofessionalise teaching.[19] However, the World Bank prefers to use a range of more innocuous terms, such as 'para-teachers', 'community teachers' or 'local teachers' which usefully disguise the low level of qualifications.

This makes training teachers about HIV and AIDS particularly problematic. How can you train teachers on this critical new issue when large numbers of teachers are not receiving any training at all – and when others are trying to cover traditional, already overloaded training courses in accelerated timeframes?

The World Bank's defence is that in-service training is the solution rather than pre-service training. Much better, they say, to put teachers into the real classroom situation and give them training as they work. There is some logic to this: pre-service training, divorced from the real world of the classroom, is not always the most effective type of teacher training. But, sadly, there is little evidence of the Bank having supported governments to build effective in-service training programmes.[20] So while pre-service training has been undermined, almost nothing has replaced it. There may be occasional one-day workshops for teachers, but something as complex as HIV and AIDS cannot seriously be addressed in just one day. There is no doubt that, in order to train teachers effectively about HIV, reaching teachers while they are still at teacher-training colleges is more efficient than reaching teachers once they are dispersed to schools across the country. But this does not seem to have been factored into the World Bank's policies towards teachers.

One person who has a very good understanding of what it means to be a teacher today in Africa is Paul Bennell, an academic in the UK who has studied the issues facing African teachers for more than two decades. He resents the way in which teachers are scapegoated for a whole range of problems. A stereotype has been constructed of African teachers as young overpaid males, who are bad educators and abusers of children. The truth is much more complex, with some remarkably skilled teachers; many women are also joining the profession, and low pay rather than over-pay is generally the norm.

Part of the problem comes from the way in which educational economists calculate the economic returns to specific investments in education. The difficulty is how to quantify the quality of a teacher. Is it based on their years of training? What if that training is poor quality in a dilapidated college divorced from real schools? Is it about the years of experience that teachers have? But then older teachers are not necessarily better at addressing issues like HIV. This commonly used quantitative approach risks producing generalisations that fail to capture the complex ways in which the quality of a teacher affects the quality of a child's learning. As Bennell observes:

At the World Bank, teachers come out as insignificant. At best, teachers are viewed as not important, or at worse, they are viewed as being the cause of the problem because they aren't teaching and are abusing girls instead.[21]

Sadly, the World Bank is not alone. Education specialists in the international donor community rarely place teachers at the centre of their concerns. Partly this is because the salary bill for teachers is so huge that aid money is insignificant in comparison. Besides, donor money comes in short-term cycles – typically over three years – so governments are reluctant to spend it on recurrent costs that they may not be able to cover in the longer term. Instead, donors focus on discrete, tangible things like textbooks or infrastructure – and end up making self-justifying arguments that these are the inputs that will make a real difference.

Bennell points out,

If you look at the way we talk about education, teachers are generally not targeted as a key area of intervention. Obviously we talk about improved teacher methodologies and we will talk about the training side of it, but we do not really get to grips with what it is like to be a teacher.

So, although common sense might tell us that no one is more important to ensuring good-quality education than a good-quality teacher, policy-makers take teachers for granted. So much so that teachers become invisible in policy debates or else only become visible when they are seen to be the problem. Yet the demands on teachers have never been greater.

Teachers are expected to do more and more: deliver better-quality education, child-centred education, HIV/AIDS education – and other people are wanting teachers to do other things as well.

Unfortunately, these growing demands are being placed on a workforce that has a diminishing status. Few people are now attracted to the profession, says Bennell:

You almost chose teaching as a last resort. Of course it wasn't always like that. In the sixties it was quite the opposite; only a privileged minority were educated and therefore being a teacher had a certain amount of prestige attached to it. But now, you are so poorly paid that if you are in Rwanda, it is more than likely that you will be living under the poverty line. Being a teacher doesn't bring in enough income, you might need to work in the evenings too. There is hardly any respect any more for teachers.

So, HIV has come at the worst time. Poorly motivated and poorly paid teachers across Africa now have a massive new challenge. It doesn't help when some people point to the teachers and say they are a 'high-risk' group. It can sound like an accusation. Young male teachers who are posted to rural areas, away from their own families and communities, are particularly seen to be a group likely to engage in high-risk behaviour. There is an implicit suggestion that they are likely to be sexual predators. But at the same time as being given this label, these same teachers are also told they should talk about sex in the classroom. Such responsibilities are not easy to handle. As Bennell observes:

You are supposed to teach your students the knowledge and skills to protect themselves from HIV. You should teach empathy, assertiveness, condom-negotiation. But won't the students respect you less if you stand up and show them a condom? What is being expected of you is unacceptable. The parents might not like it and why should you do it anyway? Everybody is on your back to improve the exam results and whether or not you teach HIV will not make any difference to the exam results, so why bother?

Bennell has studied how these same teachers grapple with the direct impact of HIV on the students they teach. This adds even more complexity to the role of a teacher:

AIDS has also orphaned many of your students. You see in their faces, they are desperate – possibly hungry, or simply lonely. But what can you do? Some people say you should now take on a surrogate-parent role, providing the psychological and emotional support these children are lacking at home.

Enough. You can't take responsibility for all your students. Perhaps it is better to turn away, switch off, create distance. Care less.

These complex pressures on teachers need to be acknowledged if there is to be any effective response to HIV. It is clear that teachers need more, not less, training – and yet the present trends are in the opposite direction. But one reality needs to be faced more than any other; that is the desperate shortage of teachers.

In rural communities across Africa, Asia and Latin America it is not unusual to find more than 100 children crammed into a single classroom with a single teacher. International statistics tend to disguise this fact by measuring average pupil–teacher ratios, but even these can be revealing. The average pupil–teacher ratio (PTR) in developed countries is 14 children to a teacher (and in reality this works out to mean class sizes of about 30). In sub-Saharan Africa, the average PTR is three times higher, at 44 children per teacher (which likewise, in reality works out as close to double that figure, over 80 children in each classroom).[22] In practice of course, national statistics also hide massive disparities within countries. Some schools in the poorest countries do work with class sizes of 30 children to a teacher – but this means that others, especially those in poorer areas, have more than 100 children squeezed into a room.

Undertrained and overwhelmed teachers struggle to maintain control in such an environment. Indeed, it takes an exceptional teacher to work effectively in such a context – and few teachers who went through teacher-training college were trained to deal with this reality.

Often it is not just the size of the class that makes it difficult to teach; children of different grades are also squeezed into the same room, a phenomenon known as multi-grading. Children in the first grade sit next to those in the second and third grades whose needs are quite different. Teachers make miraculous efforts to cluster the children of different grades together and to juggle their own time, but inevitably many children are, at any one time, left without any meaningful tasks.

There is a shockingly high number of single-teacher schools in rural communities around the world – and although some see multi-grade teaching as the best low-cost solution in these communities, the impact on the quality of learning is severe. With the abolition of school fees and campaigns to extend primary-school enrolment to all children, the number of schools with huge class sizes in now increasing, particularly across Africa. In just five years, between 1999 and 2004, the average pupil–teacher ratio in Mozambique rose from 61 to 65, in Congo from 61 to 83, in Tanzania from 40 to 56.[23] Where one would expect the trend to be towards reducing class sizes, in practice the opposite is happening. New teachers have not been recruited, even where enrolment rates have risen dramatically.

Schools that suffer from these unmanageable class sizes are likely to be disadvantaged in many other ways,[24] occupying ramshackle buildings with little light, poor air circulation and a shortage of furniture and textbooks. Children will often sit on the floor or on logs, with several of them sharing a single textbook.

What hope is there in such an environment for a child to have their voice heard if they have a question? For most teachers, the principal task becomes one of containment – taming or controlling the children so that they follow instructions. Rote learning becomes the default approach, with the teacher lecturing children rather than interacting with them. This becomes domestication, not education. Children learn more from what they do than from what they hear. In this setting they do little more than sit passively, obediently and unquestioningly.

It can come as little surprise that more and more children are failing to learn much in such schools. Every time that governments or research institutes conduct reliable tests of children's ability to read and write, the results are alarming.[25] In Ghana, on completing primary school, just 10 per cent of students reach the desired level in Maths and only 5 per cent reach an acceptable level in English, the main national language. In India, almost half of seven- to ten-year-olds cannot read at the level expected of a first-grade student. In Niger, after six years of primary school only 13 per cent of students have grasped the French language and only 11 per cent can pass a basic maths test.

This starts to undermine the case for schooling, especially for poor parents in rural areas. Poor parents send their children to school year on year in the hope that school really will be a passport to a better life. But they see children coming home, failing tests, repeating grades and failing to learn the skills that will help them in life. Indeed, children may even become de-skilled in locally relevant livelihood skills as they invest all their time in going to school.[26] For poor parents, educating children is already a gamble – as money has to be paid up front, whether for fees, uniforms, books, equipment or other charges. Now it is becoming an unrewarding gamble as children fail to progress through the grades or fail to learn.

Many people acknowledge the depth of this crisis in primary schooling across Africa, Asia and Latin America and are now rallying behind a call for a shift in focus from access and towards quality of primary schooling.[27] Even the World Bank's latest mantra is that we should focus on 'learning outcomes'.[28] This can be a positive – but not when it is traded off against access. The suggestion that one has to make a choice between delivering on the basic right to education for tens of millions of children who have never been to school, and guaranteeing a minimum quality of education for hundreds of millions already in school is simply wrong. The resources can be found – and have been promised repeatedly – to assure that both goals are achieved.

Unfortunately, this new concern for quality seems to be associated with the same disregard for teachers. Indeed, teachers once again seem to be getting the blame – it is they who are said to have failed to teach children adequately. The new concern with learning outcomes seems to encourage a focus on testing to see whether children are learning, rather than focusing on ensuring that some of the basic prerequisites are in place. The World Bank's investment following this new agenda is more likely to be spent on testing regimes and academic research than to recruiting or training more teachers.

For schools to play the role that they urgently need to in response to HIV, investment in education as a whole needs to increase – and teachers need to be placed at the centre of the equation. Without trained teachers working with manageable class sizes there is little hope that education systems will be able to play a key role in preventing the spread of HIV. Without schools that have the basic parameters for delivering quality education, no new interventions are likely to be effective.

Yet, in spite of the crisis in education there have been some excellent examples of how to make schools into effective centres for the prevention of HIV. Chapter 4 outlines some examples which offer hope for the future.

4
The Power of Prevention

We should be winning in HIV prevention. There are effective means to prevent every mode of transmission; political commitment on HIV has never been stronger; and financing for HIV programs in low- and middle-income countries increased six-fold between 2001 and 2006. However, while attention to the epidemic, particularly for treatment access, has increased in recent years, the effort to reduce HIV incidence is faltering.

Global HIV Prevention Working Group, 2007[1]

By 2015, it is estimated that there will be 60 million more new HIV infections around the world than in 2007.[2] Sixty million more infections of a communicable disease which we know how to prevent. Most people get HIV through unprotected sexual intercourse, sharing un-sterilised injection equipment (mostly by injecting drug users) or during childbirth. Each of these main forms of transmission can be prevented in different ways: sexual transmission is greatly reduced by using a condom or changing sexual behaviour in order to reduce risk; sterilised needles will prevent drug users or medical patients from becoming infected, and transmission during childbirth is greatly reduced if the mother takes antiretroviral therapy.

In the early stages of an epidemic, HIV is largely confined to certain high-risk populations: sex workers, injecting drug users and gay men (who have increased risk of HIV infection because the virus is more likely to spread through anal than vaginal intercourse). Under these types of scenarios, targeted interventions are needed to prevent the spread of the virus. Examples include providing needle-exchange banks for drug users to reduce their risk of infection. Or promoting safer-sex messages and condoms for sex workers and gay communities. This approach is called harm reduction.

In the 1980s, when HIV was first recognised, the gay community in the United States launched huge campaigns, encouraging gay men to use condoms and to reduce the number of casual sexual partners. This large and targeted campaign led to the American gay community taking control of the epidemic and stopping HIV rates from spiralling out of control.[3] HIV prevention was a great success, with the annual number of HIV infections dropping from 150,000 in the late 1980s to 40,000 by the early 1990s.[4]

In most parts of the world, HIV epidemics have remained contained within this concentrated phase and, by and large, the general population is at a very low risk of being infected with HIV. Some countries, such as Thailand or Cambodia, have run very successful targeted HIV prevention campaigns for sex workers and have been able to keep the virus under control.

The second phase of an HIV epidemic is when the virus is no longer restricted to these 'key populations' but starts spreading out to the general population, as is the case in east and southern Africa. It was previously assumed that most concentrated epidemics were likely to turn into generalised epidemics without sufficient intervention. However, it now seems that many concentrated epidemics in Asia and Latin America are unlikely to spread to the general population.[5] In west Africa, most of the epidemics are mixed epidemics, which means that HIV is still largely confined to high-risk groups but that a significant number of the general population has also become infected. Although a targeted response is still needed, a broader effort is also required to educate the general population.

In east and southern Africa, HIV epidemics are generalised and some are 'hyper-endemic' (when more than 15 per cent of the general population is HIV-positive). In these unusual situations, HIV has spread throughout the entire population and everyone is assumed to be at risk. In these generalised epidemics, the approach for HIV prevention also has to be generalised, with the aim being to reach as many people as possible. However, a targeted approach is also needed to reach high-risk groups, particularly sex workers and gay men in this case. One of the problems is that these two groups are highly stigmatised in the region and thus many governments are in denial that these vulnerable groups exist and that they urgently need HIV services.

Why is it that only east and southern Africa have had HIV epidemics which have spread throughout the entire population? Nobody knows the answer for sure but there are probably a number of reasons: these include the fact that this is one of the poorest regions in the world so the underlying infrastructure is not available to detect, prevent and contain the spread of the virus. West Africa is just as poor in many parts but the epidemics in that region are on a much smaller scale than in east and southern Africa. The reasons for this may include different cultural and sexual practices, such as the common practice of male circumcision in west Africa, which has recently been found to reduce the chance of HIV transmission by at least 50 per cent for men.[6]

What do all these different types of epidemics mean for HIV prevention? In countries where epidemics are still concentrated, it is important that governments proactively seek out key populations and provide targeted interventions. This sounds much easier than it is. The reality is that these high-risk groups faced prejudice and marginalisation before the onset of HIV. With HIV, this stigmatisation has often deepened. Few governments have been courageous enough to accept that these groups deserve the same attention and support as the rest of society. Prevention for these target groups needs also to become a political process, as will be described in Chapter 6.

In generalised epidemics, there is a need for both targeted and generalised approaches. Schools provide an opportunity to reach many young people before they become sexually active. Although viewed as a generalised approach to HIV prevention, school interventions have also been launched in countries with concentrated epidemics on the assumption that it is better to know about HIV than not and better to stop an epidemic before it becomes generalised.

Education for HIV prevention has therefore been at the forefront of the response to HIV. Education can impart knowledge, positive attitudes and skills that will reduce a person's chances of getting HIV. Although education efforts need to go beyond schools, the classroom has taken a central role in HIV prevention efforts simply because it is seen as an effective way to reach large numbers of young people who – by and large – are not yet infected with HIV.

Despite this identified potential for schools to teach young people about HIV, it has been very difficult for schools and teachers to launch the type of comprehensive HIV and AIDS education programmes that are needed. Researchers who have tried examining the impact of school interventions often find that there are increases in students' understanding but what is less clear is the extent to which this leads to the desired behaviour changes.[7] One of the problems with determining whether or not an HIV education programme in schools has worked is that we often have to rely on the extent to which students say they have changed their behaviour. This form of self-reporting is open to social biases with people more likely to say what they think is the desirable answer.

A more certain way to measure whether or not a programme has the desired impact is to measure incidence (the rate of new infections) of HIV, sexually transmitted infections or pregnancies.[8] Very few studies have done this as it is expensive and also often faces resistance from communities. One study in Tanzania, called Mema Kwa Vijana, did manage to measure these biological indicators and also used science's gold standard: the randomised control trial.

Randomised control trials are favoured scientifically because they randomly assign some schools to run the programme and others not to and therefore it is possible to compare the intervention with a 'control group'. Without an adequate control group, it is very difficult to attribute what change took place because of the programme because it is impossible to counter the argument that any observed changes might have happened without the programme.

Although better from a scientific point of view, there are serious ethical implications of this type of study: is it ethical to provide HIV education to some young people but not others? The Mema Kwa Vijana study bypassed this ethical dilemma by giving the control schools (those who typically do not receive the intervention) a much smaller 'dose' of the education programme.

Despite examining a wide range of outcomes, which included knowledge, reported behaviour changes and biological outcomes, Mema Kwa Vijana only showed an impact on knowledge and attitudes, very little impact on reported sexual behaviour and no real impact on any of the STIs or pregnancy rates.[9] The study highlights the big difference between changing knowledge and changing actual risk-taking behaviour.

In addition, there are many reasons why school interventions have not shown the desired outcomes, many of which were described in the last chapter and relate to a wider underlying crisis in education. These include:

- lack of understanding of the factors which affect sexual behaviour – especially in different cultural contexts;
- structural barriers, such as poverty and gender inequality which hamper behaviour change;
- low-quality and under-resourced educational institutions, undermining the quality provision of HIV and AIDS education;
- insufficient funding spent on equipping AIDS educators with the skills and resources they need;
- the pedagogical basis to HIV/AIDS education is weak;

- insufficient attention to international evidence on the characteristics of effective HIV education programmes; and
- fundamental disagreement on what messages about sexual
  behaviour should be delivered in schools.[10]

Despite these numerous challenges, there are many excellent
examples of approaches that are successful in educating young people
about HIV and sex and that can help young people to go beyond
developing passive knowledge about HIV.

The challenge is to make HIV a personal issue which goes beyond
an abstract understanding: to make HIV something that people
realise can affect their lives. Once people realise that the risk is real
they can then decide for themselves how they want to manage that
risk. This approach is known as a risk-reduction approach and it
assumes that rational decisions will lead to behaviour change. But
this is only part of the way forward, for this assumes that young
people have sufficient control over their lives to make these types
of changes. In many cases, this not the case: young people who are
living in poverty, especially young women, have very few choices
and very little control. HIV prevention efforts which target only the
individual and their individual risk-taking behaviour may fail to
address underlying factors and power dynamics in their community
which make people vulnerable to HIV in the first place. Approaches
which seek to address these wider dynamics are sometimes called
vulnerability reduction or a structuralist approach.

The main difference between these two approaches to HIV
prevention is the extent to which it is assumed that an individual
has control over his or her actions and the extent to which this
control is 'rational'. Academics who believe people do have control
are sometimes known as rationalists, or bounded rationalists. The
rationalist framework is individualistic, assuming that individuals
have the freedom to learn and act, to become self-autonomous and
self-empowered, and to have 'agency' over their own actions. For
HIV prevention to be effective it is assumed that an individual will
be able to act upon the knowledge and skills they have learned.[11]
While such a view may prevail in many Western societies, where the
idea of an individual being in control of his or her actions tends to
dominate, this is not the case in other countries. Instead, collectivism
and solidarity are often the norm, and an individual's self-identity
is very much incorporated within that of the group, be it family,
village, or community.

Those opposed to the idea of such individualism or self-determination are often called structuralists. In their view human action is influenced more by underlying economic, social and cultural structures. Evidence clearly suggests that young people live within a complex web of social and cultural interactions, which frame their decisions and actions. Political, economic and cultural constraints mitigate against the success of HIV prevention efforts. By focusing on the individual, rationalist approaches to HIV prevention tend to downplay the significance of these constraints.

To date, most HIV prevention programmes have been conceptualised within a rationalist or risk-reduction framework. The underlying assumption is that a person is somehow lacking in certain knowledge and skills which, if taught and learned, could be applied in different situations, thereby reducing their risk of HIV infection. Although it has been argued that this risk-reduction approach is too individualistic, the challenge has been to design education programmes which successfully address the wider community constraints which make young people vulnerable to HIV in the first place. It sounds easy to say that education should reduce young people's vulnerability in general, but how? Is this actually possible? And even if it is possible, can it happen in schools given the low quality of schools in most poor countries?

Although addressing vulnerability makes sense in theory, the challenge is how to do this in an educational programme which can be scaled-up and replicated. Some of these vulnerability-reduction programmes become so general and all-encompassing that vital specific knowledge on HIV and sexual behaviour can become lost. For structuralists, HIV prevention becomes a development issue and it is as important for them to address poverty and gender inequality as it is to deal with HIV. But if programmes fail to equip vulnerable young people with the knowledge about safe sex and HIV they need, then a key opportunity to prevent the spread of HIV is being lost. Acquisition of knowledge may not be sufficient to guarantee prevention but it is certainly a necessary part of the process.

It seems to make sense to target the individual in the short term while taking a longer-term perspective by tackling the collective.[12] The three case studies below provide successful examples of how education can be used to go beyond simply providing information, becoming something real and personal for participants and linking individual experience to collective issues. In the first case study, Theatre for a Change uses participatory methodologies to tackle some of the wider vulnerability factors such as gender and power inequalities discussed above.

THEATRE FOR A CHANGE

One way to overcome the difficulties faced by teachers in teaching about HIV and sex is to encourage teachers to recognise HIV as an issue that is important to themselves and to their students. One innovative approach to training teachers comes from Ghana.

Ghana is a small West African country with a population of 22 million people and a national HIV prevalence rate of 2.3 per cent.[13] Realising that the epidemic must not be allowed to spiral out of control as it has in east or southern Africa, the Ghanaian government reached out to civil society as important partners. The Ministry of Education has been admirably inclusive by involving NGOs in the process of designing new curricula on HIV and AIDS. In addition, noting how many disparate NGOs were working in HIV prevention in schools, the Ministry of Education set up a system to register organisations and track who was doing what.[14] Finally, the government realised that HIV must be made a compulsory and examinable part of pre-service teacher training.[15] Again, government took a coordinating and leadership role but let NGOs with innovative programmes help with the training.

One of these programmes was 'Theatre for a Change'[16] which uses drama and participatory approaches[17] to work with trainee teachers (through pre-service teacher training) in challenging underlying power and gender relations.[18] The NGO targeted this specific group as they realised that trainee teachers were not only young and open-minded, but also more enthusiastic about teaching, and less didactic. The learning process was intensive and sustained – all first- and second-year students took part in weekly sessions – each about two hours long. Trainees were then assessed at the end of the year and graded on their achievement. In total, more than 4,200 teachers have now been trained, and the Ghanaian Ministry of Education is slowly taking over the coordination of the programme so that the expertise can be sustained.

The assumptions behind the training package are that gender relations underlie vulnerability to HIV infection and therefore achieving gender equity is one of the key ways to prevent the spread of the epidemic. The training package is different to the mainstream curriculum on HIV and AIDS in that it doesn't assume that complex skills such as assertiveness can be learnt in a 45-minute session.[19] Instead, the focus is on analysing the underlying power relationships through the use of theatre.

In Ghana, the pre-service training package involved critical self-awareness of power relations through experiential learning. In other words, trainee teachers practised role playing and understanding how to change habits. Participation was taken to mean 'experiencing'; the motto was '80 per cent action, 20 per cent talking!' For many of the young trainee teachers, this was the first time they had been encouraged to develop their own opinions.

It therefore came as a surprise when they were told in 'Theatre for a Change' 'Let's be loud! Let's hear your voice!'

Trainees explored how power manifests itself in movement, space and voice. For example, eye contact reflects implicit power relations: those who are in a less powerful position are less likely to maintain eye contact. In the training, teachers were asked to maintain eye contact with other teachers and then to explore how they felt. What patterns did they notice about eye contact? What did this mean for balance within a relationship? As one trainee teacher recalled,

Before Theatre for a Change's programme, I hardly maintained eye contact during conversation with people. And now? Of course, I've improved massively on the maintenance of eye contact, which has enhanced my confidence and communicating skills. I was able to maintain eye contact with my father for considerable moments without any ill feeling for the first time. Yes, for the first time!

Male teacher trainee

Balance was used as one of the key ways to explore power relations. The trainees worked in pairs to find physical balance with one another. After much playful repositioning, standing on one leg and falling over, they finally found a state of balance. When asked to reflect on what they noticed about balance, it became clear that being in balance felt good, they felt stronger, relaxed and happy, and most importantly, being in balance required them to be at the same level as one another.

From this analysis, trainees were constantly encouraged to deconstruct relationships in terms of gender-related power. Trainees physically tried different role plays, and then were asked to report on what they had experienced. What did they notice about eye contact? What did this mean for balance within a relationship? How did this relate to teaching and learning in a classroom?

Through the use of these participatory activities, trainees experienced how power dynamics varied depending on the dominant learning methodology. For example, in a traditional formal school setting, the power dynamic often involved one active person (the teacher) while the rest (the students) were passive and not in control. While acknowledging that participatory pedagogies and child-centred approaches to learning involve a shift in power, the 'Theatre for a Change' trainees were encouraged to realise that handing over power did not mean losing power.

I would be a liar if I said I have not noticed any changes in my life as a result of Theatre for a Change. Like all changes, it crept up on me like a sandstorm in the desert – although this wasn't as harsh. Right now I see myself as more assertive and reflective of my own behaviour and the behaviour of others.

Female teacher trainee

MAKING PREVENTION PERSONAL

Starting with the teachers is a first and necessary step in providing HIV prevention in schools. Unfortunately, it is not enough by itself. After more than two decades of the AIDS epidemic, it is clear that simply giving young people information and telling them what they should or should not do is insufficient.[20] Young people need to connect with the issue and realise that they are personally at risk of HIV infection. In many countries, people see HIV as an issue which happens only to 'others' rather than to them.[21]

One problem with HIV prevention is that teenagers often do not realise that a risk (i.e. HIV infection) is real and can actually affect them. This feeling is often heightened because HIV is so hidden. The challenge therefore becomes to make HIV prevention real and personal.

In Mozambique in southern Africa, the organisation Kindlimuka has been making HIV prevention in schools personal by using educators who themselves have HIV. Kindlimuka, which means 'Wake up!' in Ronga – the local language – is the largest association of people living with HIV in Mozambique, and fosters solidarity between people living with HIV.

The Kindlimuka course ran for a year in schools but for most of this, the students did not know that the Kindlimuka educators had HIV. In order to make HIV real and relevant, the Kindlimuka educators used games to involve the children in discussions. For example, they gave out different statements and asked children to line up on either side of the room based on whether they agreed or disagreed. The children then had to argue for their position. Children could then shift sides based on the arguments presented.

Learning the Kindlimuka way was fun: there were stories, jokes and anecdotes related to sex or condoms or relationships – which the children analysed to see what they could learn. The children were encouraged to tell their own jokes and stories and then link them to the prevention of HIV. Kindlimuka also gave practical sessions with condoms – using wooden penises.

If there were students who showed particular interest in these sessions then they were given additional training to form a nucleus of peer educators – usually of about twelve people – so that they could keep the work going after Kindlimuka left.

Over the course of a year, the Kindlimuka educators built up a close relationship with all the students, becoming positive role models. It was only at the end of the year that the Kindlimuka educators told the students about their HIV status. Even though the students had learnt about HIV, it was often only through this personal realisation that they understood for themselves that people with HIV were just like anybody else.

As one Kindlimuka educator, Amos, remarked:

The government is now developing a curriculum on HIV but I am not sure this will work. You cannot teach HIV like a normal subject. It is not something you can pass an exam on. The key is to get children to internalise it – to change their behaviour – not to pass a test. Teachers will find it hard to change the way they teach. Ideally we should have HIV activists working in all schools in the way we do – but this is also hard. There are many places outside Maputo where no one is open about their positive status. It is easier in a big city where you are away from your own family.

Amos argued that nobody can speak better on HIV than those people who are positive themselves. This is a principle that was accepted internationally early on in the epidemic, when the Paris AIDS summit in 1994 established the principle of 'GIPA' (greater involvement of people with AIDS).[22] Despite commitment to GIPA, organisations and governments are still some way from meaningfully involving people with HIV in the design, implementation and evaluation of HIV programmes.[23]

There are obvious reasons for this. Only a minority of people with HIV wish to disclose their status publicly. Those who do openly disclose their status are often poor and often women, who have chosen to disclose in order to gain access to services.[24] Often they are people with little power in society, who are probably already marginalised and have little to lose by disclosing their status. The rich can afford to hide their status – treating opportunistic infections and accessing antiretroviral therapy. One result of this is that, in many countries, organisations of people who are open about their status tend to be dominated by people who are poor or marginalized and who thus lack powerful connections. This means their voice is weak and the principle of GIPA is applied in a tokenistic fashion. Another result is that HIV becomes known as the disease of the poor – which further entrenches prejudice and reinforces the silence of those with wealth and power who are positive.

Despite these obstacles there is no doubt that working with people who are living with HIV and AIDS, and bringing them into schools, can be a powerful way to break stigma and challenge prejudice.

BEYOND SCHOOLS

Seventy two million children who should be in school are not.[25] This makes the challenge of addressing HIV and AIDS greater than ever. So what do we do with the tens of millions of children who are outside of school? These are often the most vulnerable children and statistically the ones who are more likely to be infected with HIV.[26]

Ideally, all children and young people would be in school and, for many reasons, schools are the best and most trusted vehicle for teaching about HIV and sex. However, given that so many young people, including the most vulnerable, are not at school, how do we ensure that HIV and AIDS education reaches all young people?

There are of course many other ways of educating children and young people – providing them with enough accurate information so that they can make their own choices about HIV. Schools are important but equally important are television, radio, drama, families, religious leaders, pop stars, billboards, the internet, art, songs, jokes and magazines. Many would argue that young people are far more influenced by the mass media and popular culture than by what teachers say.

One programme which stands out for managing creatively to use different forms of communication in teaching about HIV, and which has also created a holistic and coordinated response, is Soul Buddyz in South Africa.[27]

In the history of AIDS, the story of South Africa is perhaps one of the most tragic. In 1990, HIV prevalence rates were the same as in Thailand but by 1998 they were twenty times higher.[28] In 2007, South Africa was the country with the largest number of HIV infections in the world although rates varied greatly between provinces; up to 39 per cent of adults were infected in KwaZulu-Natal compared with 15 per cent in Western Cape,[29] for example.

Although many other countries in southern and eastern Africa have been hard hit by HIV and AIDS, South Africa differs because of its relative wealth – the country is classified as middle-income and has high literacy rates.[30] The strengths of South Africa's economy, its human-resource base and its infrastructure mean that the country could potentially mount a response to the HIV and AIDS epidemic unrivalled by neighbouring countries.

Yet, despite this potential, the response in South Africa has been disappointing. Thabo Mbeki, the South African president, has been widely criticised in the past for being an AIDS denialist. In 2000, Mbeki made a speech at the International AIDS conference in Durban in which he refused to acknowledge the link between HIV and AIDS and alternatively said that AIDS was a problem to do with poverty.[31] For several years after, it was speculated that Mbeki was in contact with various AIDS denialists and that he himself did not believe in the link between HIV and AIDS.[32] Although Mbeki never quite admitted this publicly,[33] his office was forced to issue a statement in 2002 stating that HIV did cause AIDS.

The controversy surrounding Mbeki intensified with the appointment in 1999 of Manto Tshabalala-Msimang as health minister. She has been vilified internationally for not fully supporting antiretroviral therapy programmes. Instead, she has promoted eating garlic, lemon and beetroot as a way to help people with AIDS.[34]

The former UN Special Envoy for AIDS in Africa, Stephen Lewis, called the South African response to AIDS 'more worthy of a lunatic fringe than of a concerned and compassionate state', describing the government's attitude towards treatment as 'obtuse, dilatory and negligent'.[35]

Shortly after this public condemnation of Manto Tshabalala-Msimang , the Treatment Action Campaign led public protests across South Africa, calling for her resignation. To date, Mbeki has refused to fire this controversial political figure and has insisted that the government has been misrepresented and is now re-examining its communication strategy. Chapter 9 returns to the issue of Mbeki and discusses some of the underlying political and racial reasons which might explain why he has taken this controversial stance.

Despite the government's late response to HIV and AIDS, South Africa has been fortunate enough to have a strong and skilled civil society, which has produced some of the most innovative and successful HIV programmes for young people.

Soul Buddyz, is an offshoot of Soul City – a highly successful national television soap opera about AIDS. The programme charted the lives of several families who have all been affected by HIV in one way or another. In a similar way to Kindlimuka, its aim was to present HIV as a real issue that affects real people.

The Soul Buddyz programme targeted children aged eight to twelve, before they became sexually active and before they developed negative patterns of behaviour such as having unprotected sex. The concept was to make education entertaining, which they branded as 'edutainment'.

The Soul Buddyz were a fictitious group of twelve-year-olds who lived in Johannesburg who, although from different backgrounds, supported each other through the problems that they faced on a day-to-day basis. The children had to deal with issues such as sex, alcohol, bullying, rape and crime, all of which are also related to increased vulnerability to HIV infection.

Rather than teach about HIV in a scientific or direct way, the programme tackled the issue through real stories and through the relationship of HIV to social, gender and economic inequality. The storylines were developed through focus-group discussions with children to find out what were the more important issues that they had to face. By involving children in the design of the programme, the producers ensured that messages given by the programme reflected the reality of their target audience. Although this seems like an obvious step, many programmes fail to conduct the type of research and situation analysis needed to understand the aspirations of and influences affecting their target audiences.

After identifying the main issues facing children in South Africa, the producers identified the relevant evidence and then used artists and writers who could turn the evidence and messages into a television drama. Each episode was then piloted with young people and people living with HIV to check the explicit and implicit messages generated by the programme.

Underlying the concept of the Soul Buddyz is that solidarity can bring the love and courage needed to tackle the challenges inherent in growing up. Each problem was experienced by an individual child but resolved through the group working together. Figure 3 gives a snapshot of the introductory stories of some of the key characters.

Introducing Thapelo and Karabo
Key message: you cannot get HIV from everyday contact
Karabo lives in a rural area, where she decides to establish a Buddyz group with her new friend Ndivhuho. Thapelo, whose mother has died and whose father is living with AIDS, is one of the only children interested in joining, but Ndivhuho is against it. Ndivhuho objects to Thapelo joining because of his father's HIV status. Karabo tries to convince her that there is no danger and in the process Karabo almost loses her friend and nearly fails in getting the Buddyz group started. In the end Ndivhuho realizes that she cannot get HIV from being friends with Thapelo and they start the Massive Buddyz group.

Introducing Andre
Key message: ask for help if you have problems
After his mother's death, Andre goes to live with his uncle Tommy. Tommy is a bachelor and struggles financially to cope with this new role. Andre's school fees need to be paid, but he doesn't want to tell Uncle Tommy because he doesn't want to be a burden, especially since Uncle Tommy had just bought him new school clothes. Andre tries to raise money himself and is too embarrassed to ask for help. Uncle Tommy finds out about the school fees and sells his car to get the money. In the meantime Andre had told his friends and he finds out that he can apply for a foster care grant. He and Uncle Tommy talk and they go to see a social worker.

Introducing Bonnie
Key message: prejudice and discrimination is wrong
A new girl, Delange – a refugee from the Congo – starts at the school. She is a friend of Andre and lives in the same block. Andre asks Bonnie to keep an eye on Delange because she is in the same grade. Bonnie feels pressured by friends and discriminates against Delange. This brings her into conflict with the Buddyz. Bonnie in turn also experiences some discrimination and then realizes how she wronged Delange. She apologizes to Delange and the Buddyz with the help of her sister Avril.

Figure 3   Example storylines from Soul Buddyz. © Soul City.

The strength of Soul Buddyz was that although all the issues covered are serious and important, they were communicated in a fun and realistic way. Gone is the idea of a teacher imparting facts to a child who passively absorbs them. Although watching the television programme still didn't involve much participation from the children, at least they could connect with HIV as an issue that could affect them personally.

The television programme was a great success, reaching millions of children. However, what made the Soul Buddyz project unique was not only its coverage but also its creative use of other forms of education. In addition to the television programme, the Soul Buddyz were broadcast on the radio and used in schools.

Working with the storylines from the television series, Soul Buddyz developed books for teachers to use in primary schools. These included games and competitions – for both students and teachers. With the financial sponsorship that the television programme had generated, they were able to provide books for every child in South Africa. Soul Buddyz then partnered with more than ten different organisations to provide training locally for all teachers who wanted it. In addition, students were encouraged to set up their own 'buddyz clubs' to support each other with their problems. These peer-support and education groups liaised between the teachers and students to deal with problems in the school such as bullying or sexual violence.

For example, in one Soul Buddyz club, each week's gathering started by discussing issues around HIV and AIDS. Together with an adult facilitator, the group visited local clinics to interview healthcare workers and went out into the community to care for people who were sick and dying because of AIDS. Simple tasks such as cleaning homes, fetching firewood and cooking not only helped the ill but also developed children's understanding that HIV is real and could affect them.

A recent evaluation of the Soul Buddyz programme showed that after the first series of Soul Buddyz, two out of three respondents reported that they had watched, listened to, or used the key Soul Buddyz material. The television series also reached over one in three parents or care-givers. There was a consistently positive impact found on people's ability to talk openly about HIV and youth sexuality as a result of Soul Buddyz. The emergence of peer-support systems amongst young people was particularly striking.

*   *   *

These three case studies show the power of prevention in schools and beyond schools. In order to turn this potential into a reality, teachers need to be trained, the issues of HIV and sex need to be made relevant to young people and a range of creative approaches should be employed. HIV prevention needs to tackle both the individual's risk behaviour as well as some of the underlying factors which make individuals vulnerable.

It is all too easy to be negative and fatalistic about HIV. However, HIV prevention programmes are working. In its 2007 Epidemiological Update, UNAIDS cites five countries in Africa where there have been significant decreases in HIV rates among young people: Kenya,

Côte d'Ivoire, Malawi, Zimbabwe and Botswana. The decrease in rates among young people offers a way to look at new infections, because these are people who were probably recently infected.[36] In all five countries, research shows that sexual behaviour patterns among young people are changing over time. Fewer young people are having sex now with non-regular partners in Kenya, Malawi and Zimbabwe, Haiti and Zambia[37] – and condom use has increased in nearly every country which has been studied. Prevention can work!

5
Beyond Prevention

Schools play an important role in HIV prevention. However, in many communities, schools cannot afford to focus their HIV efforts solely on prevention. They also have a pivotal role to play in caring for infected and affected children. For many of the 15 million children orphaned by AIDS[1] the most stable part of their lives is often the daily routine of being at school. For children living in child-headed households, without adult supervision, the importance of the teacher cannot be overstated. This importance is difficult to quantify as, ultimately, it is about love and extending humanity to others.

STOPPING THE STIGMA

The city of Chiang Mai was the original centre of the Thai AIDS epidemic. Unlike countries in Africa, or even most of Asia, the Thai government has been proactive in providing testing and treatment facilities for HIV. If a pregnant woman is found to have HIV, it is normal practice to test the baby on its first birthday.[2] As a result, children with HIV are much more visible than in many other countries where parents simply do not have the chance to find out if their child has the virus or not. Here there are so many homes that have been devastated by the epidemic that teachers have had to face HIV in their classrooms every day of the week. In many cases, this has meant teachers are more understanding of the difficulties which HIV-infected children face, more prepared to challenge stigma and discrimination, and more flexible in working around periods of severe sickness and absence.

Just outside the city of Chiang Mai lives Kwanjai, an eleven-year-old girl who is HIV-positive. She lives with her aunt and her grandmother in a ramshackle one-room hut built illegally at the end of a dirt track. Kwanjai's mother died of AIDS when Kwanjai was just 18 months old.

Because of HIV, Kwanjai was regularly off school, missing between three and ten days a month. Her teacher, Ms Daopahai Buelom, knew about Kwanjai's HIV status and realised that Kwanjai needed extra support.

In the school there were six other children who were known to be HIV-positive – and many more children who had been orphaned by AIDS. It was impossible for Ms Daopahai not to acknowledge AIDS. She explains,

You don't need any special teaching skills to work with HIV. Just love the children and look after them. If they are sick, understand that they cannot come to school. Don't let any child discriminate against any other child – whether because of HIV or anything else.

Although the school was in a poor area, and catered for poor children, it was fast becoming an excellent example of how to make learning accessible and enjoyable for all, including those affected by HIV. Achieving this did not require specialist skills or new technologies but rather some common sense and basic humanity. Ms Daopahai knew all the children by name and treated them all equally. She listened and watched out for signs of problems:

Poor children are very quiet. They do not tell anybody if something is wrong so nobody knows. Some faint in class because they are so hungry. It is the duty of the teacher to look at their faces and try to understand and to talk to the student.

Ms Daopahai knew other schools were not so open about HIV, and some which went to extremes. 'There is a school where children with HIV are not allowed', she said. Although this was against the law it was not easy to prove the exclusion or enforce the law.

In her school, Ms Daopahai would not allow this type of discrimination to take place:

There was a boy who died last year and I heard from one of his parents that a girl in our school had been refusing to sit next to him. I went to the funeral and the next day we talked with the whole class about what had happened. I told them that I did not teach them to behave like this – that such behaviour was unacceptable.

Because her teacher has made such a strong stand against stigma, Kwanjai has had few problems herself. Kwanjai recalls: 'Sometimes I get a rash and a fever. But the teacher always helps. She gives me my medicine and takes me to her room to rest if I am tired. If I feel sick my friends go to get food for me.'

The contrast with Somchai's life, described in Chapter 2, could not be more acute. The difference lies almost entirely in the response of the school. If Somchai's teachers had intervened to stop the bullying and teasing, if they had followed him up at home, his life could have been very different.

In this situation, challenging discrimination in school has not just helped to address HIV. The school is a place that can and should transform children's lives, that offers a space where the inequalities and injustices of wider society are contested: a place where each child can be respected as an individual and can expect to be treated equally. This is not a question of financial resources, though most schools could always do with more. Rather it is about the conception of the school – its role in society. It is about focusing efforts on creating a fair environment for all children. This is not just a means (to better learning) but an end in itself.

There is a delicate balance that comes naturally to some teachers such as Ms Daopahai: a balance between recognising each child as an individual and treating all children equally:

If I ever have to say something to Kwanjai I am careful to do so softly and discreetly so that nobody can hear. No one should think she is different to any of the other children – or no more different than any child is from any other child.

The expectations that Ms Daopahai had of Kwanjai both acknowledged her difference and asserted her essential similarities to other children. When Kwanjai was exhausted by a bout of illness, Ms Daopahai would not expect the same exertion in sports as she would from other children. If Kwanjai was absent from lessons she would not expect the same results in exams or tests. The difference in expectation is not in itself because she is HIV-positive. It is not generalised, but rather it is specific, tied to the impact of HIV on Kwanjai's daily life. When Kwanjai is well and attends school regularly, then the expectations of her performance rise accordingly.

The way that Ms Daopahai dealt with HIV in her school was not guided by any policy or guideline. The Ministry of Education had not offered any suggestions, whether theoretical or practical, on how children such as Kwanjai should be treated. The issue had not come up in training programmes or workshops. It was not even a particular subject of attention in staffroom meetings or informal discussions with other teachers. This is not to say that such interventions would not be helpful. Indeed, Ms Daopahai would welcome additional support and advice and some other teachers actively need it. However, the essential humanity of Ms Daopahai's reactions and the basic common sense that she displays cannot easily be legislated for or formulated into a written policy.

A critical factor that helped Ms Daopahai react in this way was that there were 24 children in Kwanjai's class. This sort of pupil–teacher ratio makes it possible for teachers to treat each child as an individual. It facilitates the emergence of human relationships, in which the teachers can genuinely get to know each child and see each child as an individual. This becomes much harder to achieve when there are 40 children, close to impossible with 50 children and requiring an absolute miracle when there are 100 children in a class. Yet, as noted in Chapter 3, this is the reality for many children around the world, especially in schools serving poor communities in rural or marginal urban areas. In large classes, individuals get lost, teachers cannot build relationships with children and the whole environment becomes dehumanising. Kwanjai was therefore fortunate, not only in having a caring teacher, but also in going to a school where her teacher could get to know her and give her some personal attention.

CIRCLES OF SUPPORT

Ms Daopahai had the courage to act upon her principles to support Kwanjai, despite the potential problems this might cause with some parents. How did she do this? Through the very simple quality of human compassion. However, just a couple of hundred miles away, Somchai's teachers did not have the courage to acknowledge his needs. Although action always relies on individuals, responsibility must also be assumed at a higher level – in other words, it shouldn't just be the responsibility of teachers to decide whether or how to support HIV-positive children.

In other parts of the world, governments are now pursuing policies which can help schools become caring and supportive environments for HIV-positive students and other vulnerable children. In southern Africa, where HIV has hit hardest, the education sector is forced to take responsibility to respond to the impact of epidemic on its two major constituencies: teachers and students. Each year, the epidemic brings new challenges: education officials in southern Africa are grappling with how best to provide access to treatment for HIV-positive teachers; how to provide education to HIV-positive children who might be ill; how to protect HIV-positive teachers and learners from unwarranted stigma and discrimination; and how to offer counselling services to both teachers and children.

In this way, HIV and AIDS are pushing schools to look beyond their role in prevention to explore the role they can play in a much wider spectrum of issues, ranging from supporting treatment to providing a caring and supportive environment. This idea of schools as 'centres of care and support' has spread across southern Africa and schools are facing up to the challenge of HIV in creative ways.

One programme in Swaziland, called 'circles of support', starts with the premise that children have various circles of support that they should be able to draw from. When some of the normal circles of support disappear, for example when a child loses her mother or father, or both parents, other circles need to be reinforced. The school plays a crucial role, sometimes offering the only regular adult supervision in a child's life. Teachers inevitably face taking on new roles, even if they are not prepared to do so. How these teachers treat these vulnerable children becomes paramount. If teachers are stressed, overworked, or unable to form relationships with children owing to large class sizes, then the school can rapidly become an alienating environment and children may drop out. In contrast, if these teachers can show compassion and care then the school can become an attractive place for children to be – and children are then much more likely to stay in school.

Circles of Support in Swaziland works to ensure schools are fully conscious of the additional roles they need to take on in response to HIV. But the school is not alone on taking on these new responsibilities. The links between the extended family, the community and the school are crucial. Each circle has its role to play to support the most vulnerable children – and each circle needs to be aware of the other. Strengthening the links between schools and communities becomes crucial, so that the problems facing vulnerable children can be addressed in a more comprehensive way, drawing on the resources of both the school and the community.

BEYOND TEACHING

Circles of Support work to create a child-friendly school environment. This is not a new concept. How to create a child-friendly school has been part of the international discourse on education for decades, pre-dating HIV and AIDS. Although schools are all too often judged by exam results there is much more going on in any school than studying for tests. Beyond 'cognitive development' schools play a pivotal role in children's emotional, social and physical development.

Acknowledging these other outcomes is an important part of building a child-friendly school. Unfortunately, these other dimensions of school life tend to get undervalued because they cannot be easily measured. It is easy to do a test for basic literacy or numeracy skills, or a standardised test to see if someone has remembered the content of what they have been taught. It is much harder to devise tests to determine changes in values, attitudes or behaviour.[3]

UNICEF has played a particular role in promoting the idea of child-friendly schools. For them 'the ability of a school to be and to call itself child-friendly is directly linked to the support, participation and collaboration it receives from families'.[4] Connecting the school and the community is essential. Central to the concept is also the idea of being 'child-centred' – with the school seeking to realise a child's full potential, addressing the 'whole' child (including her health, nutritional status, and wellbeing) and being concerned with what happens to children – in their families and communities – before they enter school and after they leave.

The term child-centred has had a somewhat more troubled history than 'child-friendly', particularly with right-wing politicians and activists seeking to condemn the liberal education practices of the 1960s.[5] The suggestion is often made that being child-centred is the opposite of being 'teacher-centred' and that this involves some abdication of responsibility by the teacher, leading to chaos or anarchy in the classroom. In fact, the philosophy of child-centred learning depends on child-centred teachers, who try to create an environment which will motivate the children to discover new skills and knowledge. The teacher does not abdicate responsibility, though it is less likely that 'whole-class' teaching will be used and more likely that children will work in small groups on different projects, moving between workstations and supporting each others' learning.[6]

Clearly there are cases where any approach is abused or distorted – and some of the research literature clearly challenges the effectiveness of some of the more extreme applications of child-centred learning in the 1960s. Many of these research studies tended to focus on narrow cognitive outcomes (the things that can be easily measured), and failed to measure other more complex outcomes from schools. But they served to encourage a formidable right-wing backlash in Europe and North America that now seeks to impose direct instruction from a teacher as the only effective method of learning.[7] When exported to countries with education systems that are already in crisis, such methods reinforce existing bad practices, justifying traditional 'chalk and talk', reinforcing rote learning and supporting the idea that teachers can ignore the diverse needs of the children they teach. In the context of HIV and AIDS, this reassertion of 'traditional' methods becomes particularly damaging.

In practice, it seems important for teachers to use a whole range of approaches that balance direct teaching, learning in groups and independent learning. No teacher should be forced to opt for just one approach. But it is clear that in a world with HIV and AIDS, child-centred approaches certainly need to be part of the equation. The social and emotional needs of children who have been infected or affected by HIV need to be recognised. Moreover, effective approaches to prevention in school often depend on engaging children in ways that direct instruction or lectures are unlikely to achieve.

Another term that is widely used to signify the need for schools to recognise the diverse needs of children is 'inclusive education'. This concept emerges particularly from those who work on disability or special-needs education. Indeed the principle of inclusive education was formally adopted at a World Conference on Special Needs Education held in Salamanca in Spain in 1994. The term has since found its way into many other international declarations and its meaning has evolved. The core idea behind inclusive education is that teachers need to recognise difference – they need to work with the distinct needs and abilities of each individual child. Children cannot be treated as standardised units being processed through an assembly line into uniform products. The original sense of urgency to do this may have come from the diverse needs of disabled children, but HIV reinforces this need. The emotional challenges faced by children who have been infected or affected by HIV are ones that require teachers to be sensitive to their individual needs.[8]

One reason for the rapid spread and evolution of the concept of inclusive education is that in practice all children require and benefit from this individual attention. Teachers need to be encouraged to look at the diverse individual needs of all children whatever their background or context – and this would be the case even in the absence of disability or HIV. A global review of what we understand by 'quality education' concluded with the simple, common-sense message that schools need to 'start from the learners':

Understanding learners' needs, circumstances, strengths and capacities should underpin the development and implementation of all education programmes.

Education that is not inclusive, in the broadest sense of that term, is unlikely to bring or sustain improvements.[9]

Schools which go beyond teaching also try to be 'gender-responsive schools'; given how gender inequality has been shown to fuel the epidemic (as described in Chapter 3) this approach has particular significance in the context of HIV. The concept of gender-responsive schools has been championed by the Forum of African Women Educationalists (FAWE),[10] a pan-African NGO with national 'chapters' in 34 countries. Through a range of pilot schools projects in different countries, FAWE is developing its understanding of what a gender-responsive school should look like. At the heart of their strategy is the direct empowerment of girls, so that girls learn to speak out for themselves. FAWE has found the use of theatre to be particularly effective in enabling girls to express themselves. Taking on a 'role' enables girls to find a voice that they would never have normally. Girls need the space and time to meet in girls' clubs, collect their own data on key issues, analyse problems and find their own solutions. Without the active involvement of girls, building a truly child-friendly school is not possible.

Rose, who works with FAWE in Nairobi gives a powerful example.

In one school the girls identified a fundamental problem with the fact that there were two toilets for boys and two for girls. This seems fair – but the girls' club observed that girls were always queuing and that this meant they were often late back to class after break – for which they would be punished. They dramatised this issue for the whole community and demanded change – successfully.[11]

Although FAWE focuses primarily on empowerment for girls, it is equally important to work with boys to examine their relationships with girls and what issues are of concern to them.

Enabling girls and boys to articulate their own issues is clearly a key part of creating a supportive and caring environment in a school – which will help to create what we might call an 'HIV-responsive school'. To be worthy of this label, schools might also do many other things. For example they might become a resource centre on HIV for the community. Schools often have a far greater reach into rural areas than other services such as hospitals or support services. They can therefore support HIV-affected children by referring those in need to other support services. In some cases, schools can act as a host and allow support services to use the school to reach out to the community. In other cases, the school can become an important centre for community members to learn about the different types of support that they can access.[12]

For example, the programme Soul Buddyz, in South Africa, uses the central community role of schools to support vulnerable children in accessing cash grants. In addition to the television and school programme described in the last chapter, Soul Buddyz has also helped the government to provide a more effective and integrated response to the problems of HIV and poverty.

South Africa, unlike many of her African neighbours, has a functioning social-welfare system that gives out grants to poor people. A few years ago the government introduced a new Child Support Grant to help children from poor families. This grant could be claimed by millions of families, but uptake was slow at the beginning. Soul Buddyz developed a storyline on the grant for the television programme and then complemented this by touring the countryside, holding jamborees at schools in order to raise awareness and teach people how to apply for the grant.

In some places, the Soul Buddyz team found that the grant wasn't being accessed because there were no local welfare offices. They used this knowledge to encourage the government to establish more welfare offices in those remote areas. The net result was a very tangible benefit that reached children from some of the poorer families that had been affected by HIV and AIDS; schools became important resource centres for their communities as well as a platform for accessing government services.[13]

BODY AND SOUL

Sometimes the school is not best located to respond to all the needs of children affected by HIV. It is important to acknowledge this and not expect schools to be the only locus of interventions that can support children. The story of Phillip in the UK helps to explain one alternative.

In Europe, HIV is considered a chronic but manageable health problem. Unlike most parts of Africa, HIV is not seen as a death sentence and people on treatment can expect to live long and healthy lives. This difference is because ARVs have been available in most of Europe since the mid-1990s. Despite relatively low HIV prevalence rates and easy access to high-quality services, HIV rates continue to rise in most of Europe. The United Kingdom has one of the largest

HIV epidemics in Western Europe[14] with the number of new HIV infections doubling from 4,152 in 2001 to 8,925 in 2006.[15] The numbers are small and HIV is largely contained within two groups: the gay community and immigrants originating from sub-Saharan Africa.

In London, 13-year-old Phillip found that school did not offer him the support he needed to cope with his HIV status. He simply did not trust the teachers enough to reveal his status. Bearing such a secret at school was not easy. Although Phillip did occasionally talk about HIV with his mother, more often than not she simply reminded him to take his medicines. He did not want to add to her troubles. After all she was coping with her own HIV status and was in poor health.

Neither home nor school offered the emotional support that Phillip needed. Luckily, there was an organisation in London that provided support services for HIV-positive and affected youth. The organisation was called Body and Soul,[16] and was set up in 1994 to support women and children living with HIV. The organisation currently supports 500 children, 150 of whom are teenagers. When Phillip first found out he was HIV-positive, at the age of 11, it was Body and Soul that his mother took him to for advice.

At first, Phillip was dubious about joining a peer-support group but he was soon won over by the friendly teenagers he met there. The group sessions were about having fun and making friends but the sessions also created a space to discuss how HIV had affected their lives, about their status, about life, about death. These were issues that Phillip was used to blocking out. Although it was painful to open up about his own fears and insecurities, Phillip felt better in knowing that he was not alone and that other people were dealing with similar challenges.

Phillip trusted the group and he learnt strategies to deal with the future, positively. As Phillip remarks,

I kinda take each day as it comes. If I get sick I get sick but I learned to be happy each day. I learned to do things for people each day. That way, instead of being remembered as somebody who was very sick, I'll be remembered as somebody who was happy and who didn't really think that HIV was an excuse to pull back from life and people.

Body and Soul has helped Phillip to develop the confidence to deal with friends as honestly as possible, and to deal with complicated sexual relationships. For example, the group discussed when and how is the best way to disclose your status, and how to negotiate safer sex. The structured sessions allowed young people a space to be themselves, to analyse their situation, and develop the necessary skills to live positively and cope with HIV. Being able to share a secret such as HIV and still be accepted makes a real difference to teenagers.

Body and Soul has been trying to reach out to schools and break the stigma and silence which still exist in British schools. As part of these efforts, they produced a video to educate young people. Members of Body and Soul, including Phillip, spoke about what it was like to be affected by HIV. In a similar way to Kindlimuka's approach to HIV prevention (see Chapter 4), the video serves as a powerful tool to give HIV a human face, challenge prejudices, and show the possibility of using education to end stigma and denial. Hearing these young people talk at a human level about their lives helps to 'personalise' HIV, making the virus something that all young people can connect with.

The following are quotes from some of the teenagers at Body and Soul, recorded in their 2005 *Teen Spirit* video:

'Like, when my Mum told me I didn't believe it, I was like, "Hold on, you're not a lesbian, you're not sleeping around, so what... so why have you got it?"'

Lady Violet, aged 15 (mother has HIV)

'(If there was no Teen Spirit) I'd be locked up, I'd be quiet. I wouldn't share my feelings with anyone.'

Teenage boy

'When you actually tell someone about it and they actually accept it, it's like one of the best things.'

Teenage boy

'I think that we should all be open and say what we want about it, cos you can come into school and say, "My mum has cancer" and everyone puts their arms around you and feels sorry. But I don't want people to feel sorry for me.'

Teenage girl

Body and Soul is the only organisation working in London or indeed in the UK with such targeted support for children and young people affected by HIV and AIDS. As with Kwanjai's story in Thailand, the strong message is how peer support and education can be used positively to break stigma and discrimination. The organisation runs a number of different events that cater for different age groups. Younger children are brought by their parents or guardians and often do not know that it is specifically an HIV service: they do, however, learn how to discuss sensitive issues and become prepared for dealing with disclosure when their parents or guardians are ready. Some events are more specifically for children or young people who know they have HIV; they also have a chance to discuss their specific issues.

Peer-support groups improve the wellbeing of the members but they can also serve to give the members the confidence they need to challenge prejudice in wider society and to act as a pressure group to change government policies. For example, the community at Kindlimuka[17] was angry about compulsory HIV tests at job interviews. They joined forces with other HIV networks in Mozambique to lobby the government to create new laws to stop this type of discrimination. They held public marches and were vociferous in their critique of government. As a result of this collective action, the government passed a new code of conduct[18] which outlawed discrimination against employees (future or current) because of their HIV status.

Schools are not always best placed to facilitate the creation of peer groups of HIV-positive young people. The danger is that forming groups within schools can, in some cases, add to discrimination and stigma. No school is likely to be a completely safe environment in this sense. In some exceptional schools, it may work for a group of openly HIV-positive young people to meet within the school setting; but in most cases, however, it may be better for the school discreetly to support and enable infected and affected children and young people to link together in an anonymous space outside the school.

We have seen then that there are multiple roles that school can play in responding to the wider challenges of HIV and AIDS. They can create a space for discussion and reflection about HIV and they can build understanding and solidarity. Schools may play a role in addressing critical underlying problems relating to gender and power dynamics. Schools can also become centres for care and support, enabling children to get counselling and access services. They can be a base for outreach to the wider community. Most of all, schools can and should be environments where affected and infected children can feel safe, respected, stimulated and inspired – places where they feel that it makes sense to invest in their own future.

The capacity to do all this depends enormously on the wider context of the school: the training of the teachers, the size of classes, the availability of resources. Yet it also depends on individual teachers and their sense of humanity. For all the policies and laws that can be passed, the learning experience of a child can not determined by quantifiable indicators such as salaries or years of experience.

Each and every school has a distinct culture, dynamic and identity. Each school can choose to reinforce the stigma about HIV that is prevalent in society or can choose actively to oppose it. The choice should be obvious because stigma is based on ignorance and schools are supposed to be institutions designed to overcome ignorance. But in practice it requires active effort to create a school culture that challenges prejudice, which values and respects each child and which plays a comprehensive caring role in the context of HIV and AIDS. So, while systemic changes are certainly needed for schools to address HIV and AIDS effectively, change is also needed school by school. Individual head-teachers and teachers can make a huge difference; so can individual parents and so can the children themselves.

6
From Personal to Political

HIV is an epidemic of prejudice that feeds on other prejudices. Groups who are already discriminated against in society can be highly vulnerable to HIV infection. The prejudice around HIV then gets bound up with wider discrimination. This is one reason why the battle for HIV prevention needs to become political, because it will involve breaking direct prejudice about HIV and fighting for the rights of groups who already suffer from multiple discrimination and disadvantage.

One group who are highly vulnerable to HIV infection are commercial sex workers. They are also a group that suffers from almost universal discrimination within every society. It is therefore not enough to focus HIV prevention on individual sex workers. Rather, action is needed to tackle the underlying stigma and discrimination faced by sex workers. Here, education of a very different sort can play a crucial role.

SEX WORKERS SEIZE POWER IN BRAZIL

Proudly recognised as one of the all too few success stories in the brief but devastating history of HIV, Brazil has proved the world wrong. There are many reasons for this, including an active civil society and an early and serious investment in ARVs.[1] In terms of HIV prevention, Brazil has embraced the condom. HIV is seen as a public health issue, not a moralistic one. There is a sexual tolerance and openness, which not only makes it easier to discuss condoms, but also to accept that people are having sex. Of course, all HIV prevention messages have some behaviour change in mind; however, how much can we expect people to change their behaviour? In Brazil, there has been virtually no attempt to tell people not to have sex or to have fewer partners. Instead, they say, when you have sex, use a condom. This in itself requires a change in behaviour – but a considerably smaller one than demanding sexual abstinence.

HIV prevention efforts have also tried to break down some of the prejudices that stop people from using condoms. For instance, some

NGOs will spend time examining what reactions a girl might get from her father or husband if they find a condom in her pocket. They have also gone much further than other countries in terms of making condoms acceptable for all people and not just for marginalised and 'immoral' groups. One way they have accomplished this is by mixing messages about condoms with love. A key message has been 'if you are in a loving relationship you should use a condom'.

A key part of the Brazilian strategy to promote condoms has been to move beyond the association with HIV (which has negative connotations for many people) and to promote condom use for general sexual health and family planning. Pregnancy messages therefore go hand in hand with sexual-health promotion. This is a far more holistic approach and can be much more effective. In terms of internalising risk, people are more likely to worry about pregnancy (which has more immediate and obvious effects), than HIV (which is, in so many ways, invisible).[2]

Another reason why Brazil has been so successful in terms of HIV prevention is that the groups who have been most affected by HIV – sex workers and gay men – have each come together in solidarity to tackle HIV and wider discrimination in society. These marginalised groups have turned HIV prevention from a personal issue into a political one.

GABRIELLA'S STORY

Gabriella Leite is a woman who overturns all the images of sex workers as victims, forced into their trade because they are poor and uneducated. She is white, middle-class, university educated, articulate – and she also used to work as a sex worker. Life was not easy when she was a sex worker, she readily admits, but it would have been so different if people gave sex workers just a modicum of the respect they gave to 'normal' women.

Gabriella is fighting for that respect, and winning. When she first started out as a sex worker, she and her friends were often stopped by the police. Supposedly they wanted to protect the good public from 'dirty whores'.[3] This 'protection' meant 'breaking' the sex worker, treating her like the vermin they saw her as. Beating and imprisoning and raping her. The police were ruthless and unstoppable. Not only did Gabriella and her friends bear this brutal treatment at the hands of the police, but when they tried to get support from others, they were then subjected to the humiliation of being thrown out of public meetings, deemed unfit to mingle with normal people.

Being shunned forced Gabriella out to the margins of society and into the underworld where there was no law, and drugs and violence reigned supreme. Gabriella saw her wonderful and loving peers slowly lose all confidence in what it was to be a human being. They were constantly worn down and eventually started to believe that they deserved this treatment because they were, as society claimed, bad and inferior women.

Gabriella knew this was not right. She knew and loved these women and knew them not to be bad. But she was alone and weak and the voice of opposition was loud and strong. It was only when she came together with other sex workers that they each realised that they were not alone – that through their solidarity they could create great strength. Gabriella recalls: 'If you are alone in the world then your issues are personal, but once there is a group of you, they become political.'

Gabriella argued that if we examined why we think prostitution is bad, we quickly reveal society's underlying sexual norms and gender stereotyping about how women should and shouldn't behave in society. If society says that sex work is immoral, then it is akin to saying women – good women – should not be so sexual. There is a deep-rooted stereotyping that constructs wives as pure, virginal and immaculate. It is the sex workers who are the deviants – they threaten the very fabric of the nuclear family. Their deviance is responsible for unleashing male fantasies. It follows that the virginal wife could not be a sex worker, as she is not a sexual being.

This perception, Gabriella insisted, was a repression of women. It repressed women within marriage, denying them their full being. And it repressed sex workers – viewing them as abnormal, and reduced only to their physical being. They become pieces of meat, and not people with feelings and rights like any others. Men in this scenario were either seen as innocent victims of temptation and seduction – or they too were objectified as having overwhelming sexual needs, which only sex workers could satisfy.

The root problem, Gabriella argued, was that 'society' made judgments on who was normal and who was deviant, creating two parallel and unequal worlds, one of which was not deserving of respect. Gabriella's worry was that if we confused 'majority' with 'normality', then it inevitably leads us to judge minorities as 'other', enabling us to objectify them as abnormal, no longer people who should be treated with respect. This is the first step to enabling us to treat them as a commodity. The impact of this is felt on every aspect of life, legitimating discrimination against sex workers, effectively stripping them of their citizenship and basic rights, and condemning them to a life on the margins of society.

The key to Gabriella's analysis was how the construction of sexuality in society was intimately tied up with vulnerability to HIV infection and AIDS-related stigma. Because HIV affects vulnerable and marginalised communities, negative attitudes towards these groups are amplified as they become known as carriers of HIV. For sex workers such as Gabriella, the arrival of HIV had the potential to make life a whole lot worse. In practice it proved to be a significant turning point – an opportunity to challenge existing prejudices and organise for wider change.

Gabriella was the first person to declare in public that she was a sex worker, and the first to say that some women choose to be sex workers because they enjoy it, arguing that the freedom of earning money and choosing whom to work for and when made sex work an appealing prospect. And she was the first to say publicly that sex workers were women – as good or bad as any other women.

The idea of women choosing to be sex workers went against even the enlightened liberal approach, which tended to see sex workers as victims of their impoverished circumstances. Gabriella would argue:

Choose? Does anybody choose to work in a factory without windows? To do this work is a very personal decision, whether you get in or out. Some women choose to stay in and they deserve the respect and rights of any other chosen profession.

Gabriella started working with other sex workers, encouraging them to join her in this fight for justice. She founded the first national network for sex workers (Rede Brasileira de Prostitutas) and started meeting informally every week with a growing group of sex workers. The changes were remarkable from the start. Women thrived in the knowledge that there were other women who felt the same as them. Their self-pity slowly turned into anger. It was no longer they who were wrong, but it was society.

At about the same time, the World Bank gave a substantial grant to the Brazilian government for HIV prevention. Internationally, there was a concern that Brazil's sexually tolerant society would soon become the next AIDS 'hotspot'. Acknowledging its lack of infra-structure and expertise, the Brazilian government turned to civil society for support.[4] Inadvertently, the government sowed the seeds for revolution by helping to create a solidarity movement in the battle against HIV, with a surprising cast of gay activists, sex workers and drug users. It was unprecedented that sex workers such as Gabriella were asked for their opinion by politicians. Gabriella recalls:

Government officials and the media were talking about prostitutes and yet, prostitutes themselves had no voice, no visibility, and no power to be seen, heard or understood. Sex workers were always considered as the blame for diseases. With HIV, we mobilised ourselves to show everyone that we could prevent and fight the disease.

Prevention was the priority, but central to the prevention message was: 'without citizenship, there can be no prevention'.

'How, can a sex worker demand a client use a condom if she is being treated like a piece of meat without respect?', Gabriella asked.

This is where Gabriella found Paulo Freire's work of immense value. Freire is best known for writing *Pedagogy of the Oppressed* and *Cultural Action for Freedom* in the early 1970s – though he continued his activism and writing until his death in 1997. He argued that the internalisation of oppression by the oppressed was a major obstacle to change. People accept their fate, believe in their lack of worth and lose hope. This can be changed through a process of reflection and action, which raises their awareness and liberates both the oppressed and the oppressors.

It was clear that many sex workers had internalised their low status – as had many drug users and gay men. Breaking this was the first step. But to deal with HIV involved addressing both sides of the relationship (between sex worker and client) and addressing the power imbalance in that relationship. To do so would be of benefit not just to the sex worker but also to the client, who would be protected from a deadly disease.

Asking someone to use a condom requires exercising power – and power cannot be exercised in that moment if the wider relationship remains unchanged. If the sex worker remains objectified, is not respected as a real subject, or as a citizen, then nothing can change the dynamic of those pivotal moments when condom use is negotiated. The powerlessness of sex workers to use condoms is just one manifestation of wider power inequalities and cannot be addressed in isolation.

Freire's core ideas held as true for sex workers and HIV prevention as they did for the illiterate farmers with whom he worked so closely.

Freire showed the world the importance of using education as part of an empowerment process. One of his key concepts is called 'protaganismo'. Although there is no direct English translation, Gabriella gives a simple analogy: 'If you view your life as a stage, then protaganismo means that you take the lead role – you are the lead actor, the protagonist.'

For Freire and Gabriella, taking control of one's destiny requires a process of becoming critically aware – a process of 'conscientisation'. For Freire this was basically a learning process, an educational process, but not as we tend to think of it. Freire criticised most education as a form of 'banking' in which the supposed knowledge of the teacher is deposited in the passive learners for them to withdraw or regurgitate later in exams. This is domesticating, disempowering. It helps to reinforce the injustice and inequality of existing society.

But education can be liberating, contributing to the transformation of society. Anyone who chooses to educate has to make an active choice between the two models – a political choice. There is no neutral middle way. A liberating education has to start by respecting people who are learners, making them active subjects in their own learning. It needs to start from their reality and from giving them dignity and self-respect. This was central to Gabriella's mission with the sex workers. She knew that education would never make people into active 'subjects' if they were treated as 'objects' in the process.

Gabriella was aware that sex workers needed to take a step back from their daily reality in order to be able to see it and analyse it differently – to change the way in which they saw themselves and society.

Gabriella started working with Celia Szterenfeld, a fellow appreciator of Friere, and an activist campaigning around citizenship rights. Through their weekly group meetings, Gabriella and Celia tried to move beyond the identification of the women merely as sex workers to look at wider community issues, particularly health issues faced by them and others who were marginalised. HIV was always on the agenda as one of the priorities but was not addressed directly at first.

The programme was called PIM: 'partido integrado marginalidade' (party of marginalised people). The aim was to help all marginalized groups move from the margins of society to demand recognition as full citizens. By resituating themselves as a marginalised group, along with others who deserved a better position in society, the women moved beyond the narrow focus and hopelessness of their early meetings.

The next step was inspired more by Mao Zedong's public-health programme to get community health educators (known as the 'barefoot doctors') into the deep rural areas of China. According to a 1975 study:

A 'barefoot' doctor is a peasant who does part-time medical work. With their medical kits slung over their shoulders, they called on patients in their homes, and when not occupied with medical tasks, they worked barefoot in the paddy fields. The peasants recognised this type of doctor as their own and fondly gave them the name.[5]

Celia wanted to replicate this idea by training sex workers to become community-based health educators. They would start taking an active and respected role in the community (at least with other marginalised groups), thus also improving their self-esteem and demonstrating their ability to take responsibility. With time, it was hoped that this would allow them to take control of other aspects of their lives.

Slowly, the sex workers became a skilled cadre of 'health agents', working in their own communities. They were not 'trained' in a conventional way – which would involve being given a set of key messages on health and HIV to disseminate. Rather, they were taken through a wider, more holistic learning process, that addressed issues of health, psychology and society. They were encouraged to develop their own analysis, viewing health not as an individual but as a collective responsibility, dealing with issues such as self-esteem, identity, stigma and prejudice. A key objective was to build solidarity.

The women in the programme continue to work part-time in the sex industry, and part-time as health educators. The two areas of their work combine when the women focus their HIV and AIDS education messages on their clients.

At the time of the programme there were an estimated 5,000 prostitutes working in Copacabana alone – just one neighbourhood of Rio. Most of these women were involved in Celia and Gabriella's programme.[6] Sex workers in Rio have become highly skilled in negotiating condom use. One survey showed that within five years condom use rose from 56 per cent (in 1991) to 93 per cent (in 1997). This programme saved lives.

After sex workers were trained as health agents, people in their communities started to view them differently. They are now seen as people with knowledge and skills, people worthy of respect, people who are not just defined by their occupation. The women see themselves differently too. Earning money for the work they do in health education serves to increase their sense of self-worth. The skills they develop during the training not only improve the health of the communities in which they work, but also their own health.

Their self-esteem has been further boosted by high-profile people talking in public about HIV and about the difficulties faced by sex workers in Brazil. Gabriella explains how getting famous people involved has numerous advantages, because sex workers see an important person who has time for them, making them feel special and important too.

Of course, things are not perfect. Some clients would still prefer not to use a condom and will pay more for unprotected sex. Many sex workers are very poor and the short-term gains of having more money may win out over the long-term risks of HIV infection. But the negotiation process is different now to how it used to be – because the women feel different – and wider society has started to change how it sees sex workers.

At the community level, Celia and Gabriella's work has made a huge difference to the daily lives of thousands of Brazilian sex workers. However, this still isn't enough. The programme can never reach all sex workers. More importantly, there are wider structural constraints that continue to keep these women powerless. For Paulo Freire the eventual removal of these constraints was an integral part of a liberating education process: 'To change what we presently are it is necessary to change the structures of power radically.'[7]

For the sex-worker movement, this meant fighting for full citizenship rights for all sex workers. The fight had to become more political, and challenge the underlying structures that prevented sex workers from acting as full citizens in society.

Gabriella took advantage of the public fear over a looming AIDS crisis to galvanise political support for the sex-worker movement. She became such a famous public figure that soon the Brazilian government would not dare exclude her from any important meeting on HIV.

The political positioning of the sex-worker movement was further strengthened by joining forces with the international sex-worker movement and with other movements (such as the gay and transvestite movement). Links were also made with people working with drug users. Although these groups were often fighting for different rights, there was 'unity within diversity', because they were all fighting for the same goals of respect, citizenship and participation. Again, Freire was an important reference point:

There has to be a greater dream. Unity within diversity is possible, for example, between anti-racist groups, regardless of the group members' skin colour. In order for that to happen, it necessary for the antiracist groups to overcome the limits of their core racial group and fight for radical transformation of the socioeconomic system that intensifies racism.[8]

Once the sex-worker movement had achieved political legitimacy, Gabriella started fighting for changes to the Brazilian law, which she believed was subjugating sex workers. First she targeted the Ministry of Labour, demanding recognition of sex work as a legitimate profession. The movement organised large rallies, which drew even more media attention to their cause. After two years of steady pressure, the Ministry of Labour relented, redefining sex work as a legitimate profession.

Working closely with the international sex-worker movement, Gabriella is now fighting for a fundamental change in the government's approach to sex workers. Studying other governments' approaches, Gabriella splits countries into three categories: 1) prohibitionist; 2) regulatory; and 3) tolerant. In her view all of these are inadequate.

Prohibitionist laws are common in the US where even intent to prostitute is seen as conspiracy and carries a possible jail sentence. Clearly, Gabriella was fiercely opposed to prohibitionist laws, arguing that they drive prostitutes further into the margins of society and increase their vulnerability to HIV.

Regulatory laws are common in Germany, Austria, Chile and Switzerland, where sex work is legal under certain circumstances. However, sex work is still viewed as semi-criminal. The police are often in charge of regulating sex work, but the attitude is still one of protecting society from the sex worker, and police are therefore rarely regulating in the sex worker's favour. Police in Switzerland have to give a certificate of good conduct to any sex worker who wants to leave the profession; the documentation can take up to three years. The entire approach, Gabriella insists, may appear favourable to sex workers but smacks of containment rather than acceptance.

In Brazil, the approach is one of tolerance – similar to Canada, Thailand and the UK. Being a prostitute is not in itself illegal.

However, it is illegal to profit from the management of sex work. Still not good enough, Gabriella argues, because it is hypocritical, leads to corruption and is unrealistic. For Gabriella, nothing less than full citizenship is good enough; sex work should be treated as a legitimate profession with full worker rights. It is a continuing struggle.

Both Celia and Gabriella apply similar principles to drug use, highlighting the inadequacy of government policies that seek to prohibit, regulate or simply tolerate drug use. Rather than pass judgment, they prefer to focus on harm-reduction. If people are injecting drugs they should have access to clean needles. If they are taking ecstasy they should know how important it is to drink water. There is no use moralising – telling people not to drink or take drugs does not work. The key is to ensure that they are safe when they do so, and that it does not become an excuse, for example, for not using condoms. Celia points out:

HIV had the potential to drive sex workers, gay people and injecting drug users deeper into the margins of society. Instead, the very opposite has happened.

In most other countries, this is far from being the case. In Africa particularly, prejudice against sex workers, gay people and drug users has, if anything, deepened in recent years. Could Freirean approaches to education offer a way of addressing this? The emergence of a new approach to adult learning on HIV inspired by Freire offers some hope.

STAR

Freire's ideas of using education to empower communities to take action have also spread in many parts of Africa through an approach to adult learning called *Reflect*[9] and through an approach to HIV which evolved from *Reflect* called STAR (Societies Tackling AIDS through Rights).

STAR is similar to HIV prevention programmes like Kindlimuka or Soul Buddyz in that it allows people to participate so that HIV becomes a real issue. However, STAR goes further because it bridges the divide between the personal and political by encouraging participants to take political action to change their lives. The programme provides an example of tackling wider vulnerability at the community level rather than just focusing on the individual.

STAR looks at the interconnections between gender, rights and HIV and promotes an integrated analysis of prevention, treatment, care and support. For example, increasing access to treatment can lead to a decrease in stigma because communities see that people with HIV can lead healthy lives. A decrease in stigma can, in turn, help prevention efforts because HIV becomes more visible and people realise that it affects normal people like themselves. Similarly, if HIV testing facilities are more widely available, then more people will know their status and this can lead to increased prevention as those people change their behaviour to stop spreading the virus further.

But there is another crucial dimension in STAR, as Ugandan Maria Nandago from the Africa *Reflect* Network, Pamoja, explains:

Central to STAR is a commitment to power analysis within all discussions. If there is no open discussion of power relationships within groups, analysis often remains at a superficial level. Most obviously in this context, gender analysis is crucial. However, the aim should be to enable participants to develop sensitivity to whatever forms of power relationship most profoundly affect their lives. The key is to put people first – to give them the space, the time and the means to set their own agenda and find their own solutions. This way we can end the culture of silence and build a culture of speaking out and speaking up ... a culture of reflection and action.

STAR facilitators are trained to be particularly aware of the power relationships within their groups (between younger and older members or between men and women, for example) and facilitators are encouraged to create space for each group (young men / young women) to meet separately at certain times. By moving between sessions with peer groups and sessions with mixed groups, communication both within and between groups is improved.

Like many of the examples in this book, STAR reminds us how together we can be much more than the sum of our parts. The approach puts an emphasis on participants taking individual and collective action, so that the learning process is not restricted to the four walls of the classroom. In many cases, this action is highly political and involves people demanding their basic rights. Participants may put pressure on government offices to deliver better on promised services; they may track government budgets and seek to influence budget formulation processes; they may lobby local politicians or work with local media to investigate and expose abuses. There is a wide range of creative tactics used by such groups, but one of the ultimate 'weapons' is to take legal action as a final recourse – when rights have clearly being violated and other avenues have been exhausted.

Although it can be complicated and expensive, legal action is often a powerful way to secure change – and it has considerable potential for use in the field of HIV and education. For example, legal action may help to ensure that all children can access school; that particular groups are not discriminated against by schools; or even that all children have the right to information on HIV prevention in schools.

TAKING LEGAL ACTION

Sixty years ago, the Universal Declaration of Human Rights acknowledged that all humans have inalienable rights, 'indispensable for their dignity and the development of their personality'.[10] In general there has been steady (if not dramatic) progress towards respecting these rights in most countries, but HIV threatens to undo some of this progress because the stigma and discrimination associated with HIV has sparked new violations of rights. The late Katarina Tomasevski,[11] who was a leading voice on human rights and education, was instrumental in pointing out these human-rights abuses. She argued:

If one were to read the Universal Declaration of Human Rights with the aim of finding out which human rights have been affected by various responses to AIDS, one would see that most, if not all, basic human rights and freedoms, laid down as the common standard of achievement for humanity more than 40 years ago, have been challenged, violated, or denied in the context of HIV and AIDS.[12]

If approached from a human-rights angle, there are a number of issues which need to be addressed in relation to HIV and schools:

- Can a learner be denied admission to school because he or she is HIV positive?
- Are learners and educators with HIV protected from unfair discrimination?
- Can school governing bodies or principals force a learner to take an HIV test?
- What if a learner becomes very ill and cannot attend school?
- Can an educator be denied a post or fired because of his or her HIV status?
- Do parents or caregivers have to tell the school about the HIV status of their child?[13]

When the rights of HIV-positive people have been denied, legal action can be used to reassert their rights. Legal action has now been used successfully in several countries, for example in India and Kenya, to ensure that HIV-positive children can stay in school.[14]

In India, there are approximately 2.5 million people living with HIV.[15] In 2006, an orphanage in Kerala, India, was in the news after parents and teachers from the privately run local primary school protested about their children studying in the same classroom as some HIV-positive children.

Jacob Kurian, who worked at the orphanage, commented: 'We did not allow the children to go back because we knew they felt this way. Otherwise people might have thrown stones at them or something.'[16]

Meanwhile the school itself took direct action – expelling five of the orphans: 'Many parents came to us threatening to pull out their wards if the HIV-positive children were readmitted,' an unnamed teacher observed. 'We are helpless.'[17]

A local NGO tried intervening but the school said that if it reinstated the orphans, other parents would remove their children from the school so they refused to act. Next, Mr Baby – the education minister from the state – intervened, taking the side of the HIV-positive children and stating:

There's no change in the government position that the children should continue to receive instruction, along with their classmates, in the same school. We cannot let this happen lest it should set wrong precedents and send out wrong signals.[18]

Despite this intervention, the school still refused. As it was a private school, it did not have to abide by what the state government said. The only recourse was therefore to take legal action. A case was filed with the Kerala High Court. Eventually the judge issued a notice to the district education officers and the Parent Teachers Association (PTA) ordering the school to re-enrol the five children. In addition, the state and national Human Rights Commissions became involved and issued notices to the school, highlighting the illegality of discriminating against students because of their HIV status and threatening to take away the school's permit. Finally, after a six-month legal battle, the children were allowed back.

However, as soon as the HIV-positive children were readmitted, other parents began to boycott the school: 'Among the 65 students on our rolls, only three children came to school on June 21 and the next day none turned up,' the principal, Elsamma Mani told Agence France-Presse.

Although the children have won legal support for staying in school, the challenge remains to change the attitudes of the community.[19]

Challenging stigma and discrimination through legal action is easier than using legal recourses to address issues around the prevention of HIV. Particular challenges arise because different rights may be seen to contradict each other. How does a government balance the child's right to know about HIV (which may save their lives) and parents' rights to determine what their children should learn? Katarina Tomasevski observed:

Sexual practices are the least known and the most difficult facet of human behaviour to influence by public policies. Because a cure for HIV infection is not available, and because the infection is lifelong, it is essential to prevent its further spread. The keystone of prevention has proved to be support for informed and responsible behaviour. Informed behaviour necessitates, however, explicit information about human sexuality; yet it can be the case that sex education at school remains outlawed.

Endless legal changes have taken place in the past two decades. A number of countries have adopted laws to make public advertising of condoms possible. Courts in many countries have had to rule as to whether sex education can be provided to children so as to enable them to protect themselves from HIV infection. The abyss between forceful demands that school-children be provided with sex education as a matter of right, and denial of this sex education in the name of their parents' rights, defines the scope of the problem.[20]

This problem is not easily resolved. The majority of parents may want their children to learn about HIV but some parents may be strongly opposed to sex education – and this vocal minority pushes for its removal from the curriculum. In Kenya, a Catholic bishop recently argued that it should be parents who teach children about sex and HIV, rather than schools: 'We do not want lives of the future generation to depend on information disseminated to them at the wrong age.'[21]

Governments have the difficult job of balancing the rights of parents and the rights of children to information. The most relevant binding legal framework is offered by the UN Convention on the Rights of the Child, which has been ratified by almost every country in the world. The Committee that is mandated to interpret this convention wrote in 1996:

The Committee wishes to emphasize that effective HIV/AIDS prevention requires States to refrain from censoring, withholding or intentionally misrepresenting health-related information, including sexual education and information, and that ... States parties must ensure that children have the ability to acquire the knowledge and skills to protect themselves and others as they begin to express their sexuality.

This provides a powerful reference point for anyone wanting to take legal action – but this is not enough. Although the legal documents may make the situation clear, the right to uncensored, accurate information about HIV prevention is increasingly being undermined in the battle between ideology and science.

7
Religion Versus Science

The right of children to uncensored and accurate information on HIV prevention is enshrined in the UN Convention on the Rights of the Child. However, when it comes to sexual behaviour, the word 'accurate' takes on a whole new meaning. There have been divergent views on sex education for many decades, but in the past few years religious ideology and science have increasingly come into direct confrontation. Nowhere is this conflict more evident than in the United States.

The US has one of the largest populations of people with HIV in the world despite the epidemic still being contained mostly amongst the gay male community (53 per cent of new infections) and injecting drug users (18 per cent).[1] Although the profile of HIV cases calls for targeted interventions for these particular groups, the issue which has attracted far more attention and money is sex education in schools.

A substantial proportion of America's teenagers are having sex: 46 per cent of all 15- to 19-year-olds in the United States have had sex at least once[2] and by the time that teenagers turn 18, more than 60 per cent of girls and 50 per cent of boys will have already had sex.[3] Though teenagers in the United States have levels of sexual activity similar to levels among their Canadian, English, French and Swedish peers, they are less likely to use contraceptives and more likely to get STIs such as gonorrhoea and chlamydia.[4]

The US also has one of the highest teen pregnancy rates among high-income countries: almost twice as high as Canada and England, and eight times as high as the Netherlands and Japan.[5] The majority of these pregnancies are unintended, and nearly 30 per cent end in abortion.[6]

In trying to understand why American teenagers have such a high rate of pregnancy, researchers point to a lack of knowledge about and access to contraceptives.[7] In addition to an obvious need to provide information about contraception and safer sex, on the whole the vast majority of the American public also want comprehensive sex education for their children. Eighty-two per cent of adults think that teachers should provide students with sex education about both abstinence and other methods of preventing pregnancy and STIs.[8]

Despite more than nine in ten teachers thinking that students should be taught about contraception, one in four of them is prohibited to do so by new laws restricting sex education to teaching about abstinence-only-approaches.[9]

THE RISE OF FEDERALLY FUNDED ABSTINENCE-ONLY EDUCATION

Over the past 25 years, the US federal government has massively increased its support for abstinence-only programmes that limit the information which is provided to young people about sex and HIV.[10] Abstinence-only education is defined by the federal government in Title V of the Social Security Act as a programme which conforms to the following set of criteria:

- has as its exclusive purpose, teaching the social, psychological, and health gains to be realised by abstaining from sexual activity;
- teaches:
  - abstinence from sexual activity outside marriage as the expected standard for all school-age children;
  - abstinence from sexual activity is the only certain way to avoid out-of-wedlock pregnancy, sexually transmitted diseases, and other associated health problems;
  - a mutually faithful monogamous relationship in the context of marriage is the expected standard of human sexual activity;
  - sexual activity outside the context of marriage is likely to have harmful psychological and physical effects;
  - bearing children out of wedlock is likely to have harmful consequences for the child, the child's parents, and society;
- teaches young people how to reject sexual advances and how alcohol and drug use increase vulnerability to sexual advances; and
- teaches the importance of attaining self-sufficiency before engaging in sexual activity.

Federal funding for abstinence-only education has risen from $9 million in 1997 to $176 million in 2007 with the actual amount of money spent on abstinence-only education being much higher because individual states are expected to match federal funding with their own funds.[11] Although federal funding for abstinence-only education has existed for over 25 years, it is only since the election of George W. Bush and the Republicans in 2000 that federal funding has sky-rocketed. Since 1998, over $1.5 billion in state and federal funds have been allocated for abstinence-only programmes.[12] There are three federal programmes dedicated to funding abstinence-only education: Section 510 of the Social Security Act (Title V), the Adolescent Family Life Act's teen pregnancy prevention component, and Community-Based Abstinence Education (CBAE).[13] However, whether or not schools actually end up teaching abstinence-only education depends far more on the state and district government. Currently, 35 states mandate some form of sex education or HIV prevention in schools, but their laws tend to be very general and it is usually up to the district or the school to set their own policy.[14]

Given the relative freedom for schools and individual teachers to choose their own policy on sex education, the result in the classroom is often chaotic, with different students receiving different types of information.[15] And with almost all the federal funding going to abstinence-only groups, the choices teachers can make are narrowing rapidly. Essentially, an undercover privatisation of sex education is taking place all over America.

The change in American policy and practice to abstinence-only education has occurred very rapidly and on a huge scale: In 1988 only one in 50 teachers taught abstinence-only. In 1999, this figure was one in four.[16] What has been the impact of this huge change in American policy? Does this approach work for preventing HIV? The following case study is from the state of Florida and provides some real examples of what drives abstinence-only programmes. These programmes are now being exported abroad and the second case study shows the impact of US-exported abstinence-only programmes in Uganda.

VIRGINITY – FLORIDA ABSTAINS

Although all states in America have seen huge increases in funding for abstinence-only education, it is in the southern states – which are traditionally more socially conservative and religious – where abstinence-only education has found a strong foothold. More than 50 per cent of districts in the South have an abstinence-only policy whereas in the northern part of the country it is about one in five.[17]

In Florida, in the far south-east of the country, federal funding[18] for abstinence-only has been used to support a mushrooming number of faith-based organisations to start up programmes such as Managing Pressures Before Marriage, WAIT Training, Sex Can Wait, Choosing the Best Life, Reasonable Reasons to Wait, ABS Works, Capturing the Vision, Responsible Social Values, and Vessels of Honor.[19] So what does an abstinence-only programme actually look like? In one secondary school near Pensacola in north-west Florida, a group of peer educators come once a week to provide abstinence-only education to 13-year-olds. The peer educators start the class by singing a song about the joys of life and cherishing oneself. They then take out a plastic cup and ask each student to spit in it and pass the cup around. The last person in the group is told to drink all the spit. At this final request, the 13-year-olds all scream in disgust, and refuse to do so. It was at this point that the abstinence educator tells them that this is what it is like to marry someone who has been having sex before marriage as they are contaminated with the bodily fluids of other people.

This activity is followed by similarly graphic but inaccurate analogies. The educators draw a picture of a minute sperm swimming through a large gaping hole in a condom. In another game, a girl and a boy pretend that they are getting married. The girl opens the bag, says 'I have a present for you', and took out a large, mouldy cauliflower. Again, the students are disgusted; the abstinence educators ask them if they want to have sex before they marry and then give human papilloma virus (HPV) to their husband? Waving the mouldy cauliflower in the air, they proclaim how HPV could get as big and ugly as the cauliflower and would they want that dangling between their legs?

HPV, commonly known as genital warts, is an unpleasant ailment, but certainly not life-threatening, and it certainly never develops into warts the size of a cauliflower. Some strains of the virus are associated with cervical cancer and as HPV is passed through skin-to-skin contact, the abstinence groups have found a powerful message because condoms are not very effective in protecting against the virus.[20] Abstinence was therefore the only way to prevent HPV and consequently cervical cancer. However, with the introduction of a powerful new vaccine,[21] the health scare associated with HPV is now out of proportion to the severity of the problem.

The peer educators also have a strange way of using numbers:

People on average have sex 4.5 times a week. If you get married as a virgin when you are 25 then you can have sex in the morning, sex in the evening – in fact if you live to 75 you will have sex 19,500 times! But if you had sex with one random guy then you might get AIDS and then there would be no husband, you would die. And just think, you would have had sex one time and died instead of 19,500 times!

The messages rely on fear tactics and the underlying assumptions are all based around irresponsible teenagers who have to resist the evil temptation of sex before marriage. At one class, the abstinence educator argues that if teenagers can not even manage to put the cap back on the toothpaste how could they be expected to use a condom properly? The implicit discourse is that sex is bad and something to be avoided. The positive and pleasurable dimensions of sexual relationships are ignored and yet, again, there is a huge gulf created between what young people are taught in school and the reality of their personal lives.

To abstain from sex, students are taught how to set boundaries and to develop 'refusal skills'. In one training workshop organised in Florida, Mark, the trainer, explains that young people are always looking for the easiest solution and that abstinence was the easiest and only way to stay baby-free, STI-free and worry-free. Mark explains the concept of setting boundaries:

I'll give you an example of setting boundaries. Now imagine if you had a school and the children were playing in the playground but there was no fence. Where would they play? They would stay huddled up near the school because they would be scared to stray too far away into the unknown. Now imagine that there was a fence. The children would now play anywhere and everywhere because they feel safer. So it is the same with sex – when you have boundaries then you have the best sex and a lot of freedom.

In order to give a real-life example, Mark goes on to explain to the group how, when he was at college, he knew that kissing would lead to sex so he never let a girl enter his room. Mark felt that he had to set the boundaries so far back because otherwise he might 'fall off the cliff'. This meant that during his entire time at college he refused to go to the floor above his because that was where the girls were. He also argued that young men should not masturbate as that would lead to 'other things'.

Offering himself as the ultimate example of how successful abstinence-until-marriage is, Mark projects a massive ten-foot-high photograph of himself with his beautiful wife, explaining how she was a virgin before they married and how, because he waited, he got himself such a beautiful wife. He then goes on to affirm that they had great sex and that the best thing was that she did not have to compare him with anyone else.

One of the biggest criticisms about the abstinence-only approach is the gender stereotyping which portrays boys as desperate for sex and girls as having to protect their chastity or else become 'spoilt'. At one point, Mark explains to the group that HPV was easily preventable 'if only women kept their pants on'.

He continues:

Girls have a lot of power but as soon as a girl sleeps with a guy she gives her power away. Girls give guys what they want but they will get burnt by sex. After all, why would you ever buy a cow if the milk is free?

Underlying this gender stereotyping is the assumption that it is a woman's responsibility to constrain her sexuality and that men are constantly tempted and can't control themselves, as another of Mark's graphic analogies demonstrates:

You see men are like microwaves – 'Ding!' and they are ready to go. Whereas women are like crockpots, they take longer to warm up. The problem with men is when their brain goes somewhere else. Which is why Playboy sells and Playgirl does not sell. Men have got to win the battle between their brains and their dicks.

Nancy Kendall, a researcher into the abstinence-only programmes in Florida, found that the majority of messages on virginity were directed at girls. At one abstinence rally that Nancy attended, over 90 per cent of the teenagers present were girls, and in a classroom at another school the lesson had been so directed towards the girls that at the end she heard a boy ask if it was possible for boys to also get STIs. The only message that she heard directed at boys was around financial responsibility and how, if they got a girl pregnant, they would have to pay paternity cover. In one classroom, the teacher told the male students that they would pay for the rest of their lives, never being able to buy the SUV or house that they wanted.[22]

To Nancy, these traditional gender stereotypes smacked of social conservatism, as she points out: 'Fundamentally the implicit discourse is that women should be at home (in the private sphere) and men out working in the public sphere – that old distinction!'

Essentially, the people behind the abstinence movement are the same extreme social conservatives who rallied against sex education in schools in the 1970s. Bizarrely, these same groups are now becoming the biggest providers of sex education. They have manipulated the discourse to talk about women's empowerment being achieved through abstinence, when really they are promoting women's disempowerment. One such 'empowerment' programme is near Tallahassee in northern Florida. For Peter, the coordinator of the programme, the problem is not to do with HIV but rather issues of empowerment and the underlying factors which motivate American teenagers:

The media pumps so much information saying 'if you drive this, if you dress this way, if you look this way, you are going to have a good life and everything is going to be happy'. And so they do that. They buy the right clothes, they have the right friends and then they are not fulfilled. And then they get to the point and they say 'I've tried everything' and this is happening at 14. I've tried it all and life still isn't what I want it to be. So, they think, 'If I let the guys have their way with me then all the guys will like me and I'll be popular' and stuff like that. 'If I just try the right drug, I'll find happiness'.

Peter's abstinence programme is similar to other programmes in Florida where the focus is not just on sexual abstinence but on a wider, more radical change in attitudes and values; these range from what an individuals' purpose is in life to issues around self-esteem. Underlying Peter's approach is the concept of redemption. If a teenager has had sex, he or she can 'reclaim' their virginity by not having sex for at least a year. The subtext was that sex is a sin for teenagers – but that even a sinner who has strayed can be redeemed.

Indeed, many of the testimonies in the programme have a certain formulaic pattern running along the lines of 'I was on a bad path and then I discovered abstinence and my life changed'.

Despite smacking of evangelism, Peter strongly denies that abstinence has anything to do with religion at all. It is rather, all to do with promoting family values and public health:

Our approach lends itself more to a group of people who feel that the family is the basic building block for society. I think it happens that way because most conservatives feel that the family is the building block and when you start tearing down the family, society starts to crumble.

All the staff at Peter's organisation are Christian yet he argues that this is a coincidence because it was only the Christians who have the compassion needed to help vulnerable young people. How could it be that the principles, people and views promoted by the project are Christian, but the project itself is not Christian?

According to most abstinence groups, their work is about public health and not at all about religion. However, the way they talk about it betrays different concerns. As Peter explains: 'we equip them with the skills but they know that deep inside of all of them, they know that having sex isn't really what they should be doing. We're not trying to sell them anything. We're trying to tell them the whole truth.'

Despite the rational and scientific arguments that the abstinence groups employ in their campaigns, there clearly is an underlying moral agenda. The abstinence educators believe that it is morally wrong for people to have sex before marriage. Arguing for abstinence is a way to push for a return to traditional family values. This has been a familiar message from the religious right for years and it has not changed with the passage of time.

In an unguarded moment, Peter admitted that one of the main reasons that his programme started up after-school clubs was because they were not allowed to evangelise in the classroom due to constitutional barriers separating religion and the state. Setting up after-school clubs was a way of reaching students without facing these constraints:

We do encourage them to find a place where they can draw strength from other people. There were lots of times when I could not share my faith and people would say to me, you're so happy all the time, why do you have so many friends? And I wanted to say, 'You want to know where you could meet lots of friends? Go to church!'

Sometimes it is very difficult because you know the answer. You know there is a problem and this problem requires a certain amount of strength to overcome. And you know the source of strength to overcome that problem but you are not able to directly tell them. It's as if you have a disease and I have this pill here that is going to address your disease but I am not allowed by the state to give you the pill.

In effect, Peter was using HIV – a serious public health issue – to promote his own faith. The agenda was explicitly about public health but implicitly about proselytising. The after-school clubs were where the real 'education' was happening.

THE ROLE OF SCIENCE

Many aspects of the abstinence-only programmes are highly duplicitous. As well as masquerading as a public-health programme, the groups involved have misappropriated the evidence to make a scientific case for abstinence-only programmes, as Nancy Kendall explains:

I think they have adopted the discourse of data-driven decision making and evidence-based programming. But these are people who come from a tradition of really not trusting science. These are people who rant against scientific humanism regularly. I hear them say quite often, 'data can be made to say anything'.

The people behind abstinence-only programmes are driven by a deep moral conviction, and consequently they believe that what they are doing cannot be anything but correct. However, as we live in an increasingly scientific and rational world, these religious groups have superficially embraced science in order to produce the scientific evidence needed to promote their programmes. Nancy laments:

The truth is that these organisations don't care if they are effective or not in relation to STDs so long as they get some conversions out of it ... saving souls is more important than saving lives ... but they can't say that.

In her many interviews with abstinence groups in Florida, Nancy found that many groups had been given guidance from national organisations about which messages and researchers to use. The abstinence movement – as it was referred to by some abstinence educators themselves – has even set up their own research centre called the Medical Institute for Sexual Health. Ostensibly a scientific organisation, the wording on their home page suggests a remit beyond science: 'Education. Science. Character.'

So what does the evidence show? One piece of evidence which the abstinence-only groups promote heavily is the recent decline in teenage pregnancy rates. However, studies examining what has caused the decline suggest that only about 14 per cent of the decline observed between 1995 and 2002 was due to teenagers delaying sex or having less sex. The remaining 86 per cent of the decline was due to an increase in contraceptive use.[23]

Despite abstinence groups funding their own evaluations, there still is no evidence that abstinence-only education has any positive impact on teenagers in the long term. Moreover, recent research shows that abstinence-only programmes make it less likely that those who have sex will use contraception, thus increasing their risk of unintended pregnancy and STIs.[24]

In contrast, systematic reviews of the evidence show that comprehensive sex education programmes which include information about delaying sexual debut and safer sex for those who are having sex can help delay the onset of sexual activity among teenagers, reduce their number of sexual partners and increase contraceptive use when they become sexually active.[25]

In the most recent study of abstinence-only programmes, reported in the *British Medical Journal*, a team from Oxford University studied 13 trials involving over 15,000 people aged 10 to 21. They found that abstinence-only programmes had no impact on the age at which individuals lost their virginity, no impact on the number of sexual partners, no impact on rates of sexually transmitted diseases and no impact on the number of pregnancies.[26]

In conclusion, there is no evidence that abstinence-only programmes have any positive long-term effects on sexual-health outcomes. However, abstinence groups continue to draw evidence from a limited number of biased studies.

The hypocrisy in so many arenas is overwhelming. These are the same people who, during the Clinton administration, argued for less government intervention and more personal privacy. This traditional anti-government stance all but disappeared with the advent of the Bush administration. With more money and power, the social conservatives reversed their position, suddenly becoming pro-government, pro-federal government and pro-sex education. Members of abstinence-only NGOs in Florida admitted that they were all taking full advantage of Bush's term in the White House to create enough momentum behind their religious and cultural revolution so that the movement would be strong enough and would have permeated enough schools to survive and flourish despite a change in government. One government official even likened it to being near the 'tipping point'.[27]

Unfortunately, the abstinence work is part of a much larger conservative movement which extends far beyond American borders. These policies are now being exported to Africa. Have the extremely conservative views of the religious right found a receptive audience on a continent where the feminist movement is barely off its feet?

EXPORTING MORALITY

In 2003, the US Congress approved $15 billion over five years for President Bush's Emergency Plan for AIDS Relief, known as PEPFAR. This is the single largest contribution from any one country to fight HIV and AIDS. The aims over the five years include putting 2 million people on treatment and preventing 7 million new infections.[28]

Although the programme has been very successful in increasing access to treatment, the prevention programme has been criticised internationally for being driven by the abstinence-only agenda and for reducing the potential role of condoms in preventing HIV. Originally, 20 per cent of PEPFAR money was earmarked for prevention and, within prevention, at least one third had to be spent on abstinence-until-marriage programmes.[29]

PEPFAR has based its prevention programmes on the ABC model (A = Abstain; B = Be faithful and C = use a Condom), that had been pioneered in Uganda. This has been a very popular model for HIV prevention although critics argue that it misses out groups of people such as injecting drug users, and oversimplifies sexual behaviour. For example, there is nothing about a reduction in the number of concurrent partners or a reduction in casual sex partners (both of which are thought to be instrumental in decreasing HIV rates in southern Africa).[30]

Putting aside criticisms that this model is limited in the options it offers people, over the years the ABC model has been interpreted differently in different contexts. In many countries, it was interpreted as choosing from A: abstaining, B: being faithful or C: using a condom. In other circumstances, it was interpreted as abstain as a first choice, if that is not possible then be faithful and if that is not possible, use a condom.

With PEPFAR the balance between A, B and C shifted to overwhelmingly A=Abstain until marriage, with B focused on being faithful in marriage and C relegated to use only for high-risk groups.[31]

In the strategy, condom use should only be promoted for at-risk groups as a form of risk-reduction which must complement the core activity of risk-elimination (abstinence).[32] Throughout the strategy, the only choices available to young people are increasing abstinence until marriage, delaying first sex, reducing the number of partners, and achieving 'secondary abstinence' among sexually experienced youth (when young people reclaim their virginity by not having sex for a set period of time – usually at least one year).[33]

These abstinence-based prevention strategies have now been exported to countries across the world. Out of all of these countries, it is Uganda, where ABC was originally conceived, which has been most in the spotlight. It was one of the first success stories in terms of HIV prevention, and the US government has been keen to claim part of this success and turn the country into a model PEPFAR country.

Beatrice Were, an AIDS activist in Uganda, is dismayed at how PEPFAR has influenced her country's approach to HIV prevention by repackaging and distorting the ABC approach.

In the process the US government has changed what abstinence means. We used to encourage abstinence in the sense of delaying sexual debut. Delay having sex until you are mature enough to make a decision – until you are responsible. In the meantime we made sure we gave full information about sex and sexuality, including the use of condoms. Now abstinence means abstain from sex until marriage and only have sex in marriage. This is being promoted as the only 100 per cent secure way of preventing infection.

Beatrice, for one, is living proof that this model does not work. She was a 19-year-old virgin until she married and she only ever slept with her husband. But in 1991 her husband died from an AIDS-related illness and she discovered that she was HIV-positive. It is now thought that married women are currently among the most vulnerable groups for HIV infection in generalised epidemics such as in Uganda. Research suggests that married women are less able to negotiate condom use with their husbands who may have had extramarital partners and who, consequently, may have become infected with HIV.[34] The ABC model does not cater for these women.

PEPFAR explicitly supports faith-based groups to undertake HIV prevention work. In Uganda, this has resulted in a mushrooming of evangelical groups which, Beatrice argues, are just interested in proselytising and have no regard for the harmony which previously existed between different faiths.

Now it is very different. There is a new generation of evangelical groups that have sprung up with the PEPFAR money – groups that never worked on HIV and AIDS before. There used to be mutual respect – but this new abstinence-only movement has shattered the consensus.

Beatrice saw how the American evangelical groups were building a strong support base in Uganda where, she argued, young people were attracted by the prospect of being part of an American church where they could perhaps get some money or even a visa to the United States. The congregation sizes therefore increased and the churches could use this to access more funding from American churches. In addition, 'virginity parades' became a commonplace event on the streets of Kampala:

Virginity parades are incredible. Scholarships are promised to young people if they promise to abstain. But of course there is no proof! So people just have to act as if they are virgins – it is a performance. But the very suggestion that access to university is based on your sexual behaviour is outrageous. Where is the justice in that?

Beatrice has also found that the evangelical groups openly lie about HIV:

They make preposterous claims to attract people – they claim they have a cure for HIV. These evangelicals announce on public TV regularly now that HIV can be cured ... They make ridiculous claims to increase their congregation. People will carry patients to the churches in desperate hope. This is what people want to hear. Who would not want to believe? But there is real danger here. They persuade people to stop taking ARVs. This will kill people, not save them.

One of the main reasons that PEPFAR has had such an impact in Uganda is because of strong support from President Museveni and his wife. Funded by PEPFAR, the First Lady has started her own large-scale initiative on abstinence-only education and has led virginity rallies and parades.

The first lady is a born again Christian – but she was never vocal on AIDS until 2003 when Bush came along. Lady Museveni is strongly linked to these American evangelical groups. When I was in the US I was amazed at how much she is worshipped – these US evangelicals praise her all the time. Now she is the figurehead of the abstinence-only approach. And of course she has political power – it is very hard for activists and people who work in public health or the Ministries to say anything that contradicts her.

Beatrice was even more disappointed by the President's transformation:

Sometimes I feel HIV is being used as a tool to make us powerless – ignoring what we know ourselves and our values and culture – and manipulating our political leaders. Look at President Museveni – some influence undermined a strong man who was once a great role model. How can he have changed? It is simple: he came under very powerful influence from President Bush. He needed the political support of the US to stay in power ... and so submitted to their single-minded agenda.

In 2001, before PEPFAR, President Museveni launched an ambitious plan to create a national HIV prevention curriculum that would reach every child in every school. His initiative was called PIASCY: the President's Initiative on HIV/AIDS: Strategy on Communication to Youth. The process of developing the curriculum involved a wide range of stakeholders, including religious leaders. Given the urgency of the HIV epidemic, the groups reached consensus and agreed upon a set of teacher manuals that the President personally launched in early 2003. The manuals were designed for the full range of age groups in Ugandan primary schools (where many students are teenagers) and included prevention messages on abstinence (supporting girls to say no), the importance of being faithful in relationships and approaches to safe sex, including the use of condoms.

Before the new materials were printed, new evangelical groups who had not previously been involved in the development of the materials demanded the removal of diagrams that illustrated sexual organs. They insisted on a rewrite based on ethics and morality. Where the manuals advised teachers to acknowledge that some of the older children in their class would probably be having sex, the religious leaders demanded that such children 'should be told to stop'.[35]

The materials were withdrawn from circulation and the US government assisted in developing a new set of materials which placed sex as an activity which was only acceptable within the confines of heterosexual marriage.[36]

There was a new and strong focus on morality and religion, with sex seen as a gift from God that must be protected and respected. Any sex outside marriage was a sin. Presented in this context, HIV and AIDS appeared as a form of punishment for sinful behaviour. The implication was that only those who indulge in bad things are at risk – a significant move away from previous Ugandan campaigns that emphasised that everyone was at risk. There was no mention of safe sex or condoms (except in a limited way in one manual for the oldest students).[37]

In 2005 Human Rights Watch published a report suggestively titled 'The Less they Know, the Better'[38] condemning the abstinence-only programmes in Uganda. The report cites multiple incidents in which teachers were told not to talk about condoms despite realising the reality that many of the students were already having sex. A head-teacher in Mbale emphasised the absurdity of the situation: 'around here people don't buy this idea of abstinence – because in Uganda many girls are using sex to buy their daily bread.'

This echoes Beatrice's concern:

This whole abstinence-only agenda is based on falsehoods. They target girls but they never talk about gender and power relations. Girls are told to abstain but boys in our culture are still encouraged to explore – and to experience different sexual relations. Male promiscuity is socially accepted or even expected. You are stigmatised if you are a man who claims to abstain. Male virginity is mocked. This whole abstinence agenda is profoundly out of touch with cultural and social norms in Uganda and makes no attempt to address them.

The impact of the abstinence-only HIV prevention programme in Uganda is difficult to ascertain although UNAIDS suggests that the new approach is not working. Prior to the introduction of abstinence-only programmes, Uganda had been the first country in sub-Saharan Africa to show decreasing national rates of HIV. From 1992 onwards, HIV rates began to fall and then stabilised in the early 2000s.[39] Despite the levelling-off of prevalence, UNAIDS reports that there has been an increase in risk-taking behaviour, especially in the number of people not using a condom and urges Uganda to 'revive and adapt the kind of prevention efforts that helped bring Uganda's HIV epidemic under control in the 1990s'.[40]

The Human Rights Watch report cited above concluded that although studies showed no long-lasting positive impacts from virginity pledges or abstinence-only education, both the US and Ugandan governments had ignored these studies, choosing to highlight misleading survey data which suggested that abstinence and fidelity were more successful than condom promotion.[41]

Although the evidence does not support the introduction of abstinence-only programmes for HIV prevention, unfortunately, religious ideology has won this battle over science, good public health and effective sex education.

8
The Politics of Aid

There are currently more than 33 million people with HIV in the world and more than 70 million children out of school. These challenges are enormous. As it is mostly poor countries where education systems are weakest and AIDS is worst, the global response has come from the international development sector or aid industry. In 2007, the vast majority of funding for both AIDS and EFA (Education For All) came from bilateral and multilateral donors.

International funding influences every aspect of global HIV prevention, from who is targeted, what options they are given to prevent HIV and how prevention programmes are implemented.

NO MONEY FOR 'BAD PEOPLE'

HIV exposes deep moral divisions between those society deems to be 'good people' and those who are seen as 'bad people'. In order to prevent HIV, many countries will need to have the courage to admit that certain marginalised groups in society do exist, have the same rights as other citizens, and need support for HIV prevention. These groups are those who are already marginalised and also especially vulnerable to HIV infection: sex workers, gay men and injecting drug users, among others. This book has argued consistently that in order for HIV prevention to be successful, the response has to become politicised in order to deal with the double stigma towards HIV and these marginalised groups.

Internationally, aid for HIV prevention has been politicised but often in ways which make it less – rather than more – likely that countries will provide HIV prevention services to those in need.

Through PEPFAR and other international development funding, the US government has a huge influence over HIV prevention in poor countries. Apart from the disastrous push for abstinence-only approaches, which were described in Chapter 7, in 2005, the US government created a new law which prevents any organisations that receive American funding from supporting sex workers. This legislation prohibits the use of US aid to promote or advocate the legalisation of prostitution or sex trafficking. In addition, there is a requirement that any organisation receiving funding for HIV has an official policy which opposes prostitution and sex trafficking.[1]

Outraged by the new law, the Brazilian government returned $40 million of aid to the US government. Most countries and organisations, however, have not been able to afford to reject US funding and have been forced to end their HIV prevention programmes for sex workers.[2] The condemnation of sex work extends beyond US funding so that even if an organisation is receiving non-American funding for its sex-work programme, it has to stop this work or risk losing American funding.[3] Apart from undermining efforts to support sex workers, the policy has created endless bureaucratic hurdles and confusion as international organisations have to ensure that all their local partners also sign this 'loyalty oath'.[4]

In Uganda, Beatrice Were (see Chapter 7) has noticed how it is often the fear of repercussions from the US that is the worst effect of PEPFAR:

Organisations taking PEPFAR money have to stop doing all this other work for fear of losing their funding. It becomes a nightmare for people, juggling their work and how they present it to different people – and there is a deep fear of legal action. This is paralysing people and organisations.

Beatrice noticed that organisations either had to accept the sex-work policy and abandon HIV prevention services for this vulnerable group or else take the money and 'fly under the radar'. She regards the American condemnation of sex work as completely hypocritical. She once had the opportunity to meet Randall Tobias, the former head of PEPFAR, on television. Beatrice recalls,

He was smart, eloquent, convincing, but wrong ... I recall that he was particularly articulate in condemning the whole sex industry. It was only much later that I found out that this was another example of deception and pretence.

Only a few months after the interview, Tobias was publicly shamed for having been in contact with a local sex worker.[5] Beatrice argues:

It is all about pretence. Tobias was one person in the daytime and another at night. It just shows that you can't judge human behaviour on what is said. You need to go deeper. Real education about HIV needs to lead to behaviour change and that will not happen with a superficial, dogmatic programme that is based on deception.

Following the scandal with the sex worker, Tobias resigned from his position at PEPFAR; the US government, however, has not backed down from its position on sex work.

Given that some rich governments have been using the power of money to dictate who gets support for HIV programmes, it seems obvious that this is where multilateral and UN agencies should take centre stage. The United Nations should take the global leadership on HIV and ensure that recommendations and responses to HIV prevention are based on good evidence and respect for the human rights of all people.

Unfortunately, the politics of aid prevents the UN from taking this strong leadership role. Rasheed, a UN diplomat in South East Asia, argues that the neutrality of the UN renders it unable to take the leadership needed on HIV:

You need to take positions on HIV but the UN is not good at that. Everything at the UN depends on consensus. All member states have to sign up – even though, of course, some member states are more vocal than others. This makes it hard to take leadership on an issue – you can't stand up and speak out because you can't criticise any member government.

Despite receiving huge amounts of funds for HIV prevention and having played a key role in raising awareness of HIV as a global issue, the UN has been noticeably silent on issues such as sex workers, drug users or men who have sex with men. UNFPA is supposed to lead on sex work and HIV but has not been able to get consensus on a UN-wide position on the issue when formulating policy. There are polarised positions between those who accept sex workers and promote their equal rights to services, and the other extreme who argue that the response should aim to abolish sex work. The policy was drafted and redrafted. The final policy, which was presented to UNAIDS partners, met with public condemnation, particularly by the Network of Sex Work projects:[6]

The UNAIDS paper combines some of the most repressive approaches to sex work and HIV, ones that do little to empower sex workers to protect themselves but instead stigmatise sex work more and make working conditions even worse.

The paper was criticised for confusing consensual sex work between adults with issues of trafficking and child sex work. UNFPA has since retracted the policy but to date has not yet been able to reach agreement on a position which is acceptable both to countries such as the United States and to sex worker support groups.[7]

Similarly, gay men are a population highly vulnerable to HIV infection and also a hidden part of society in many countries, particularly in Africa. Homosexual relationships are still illegal in 70 countries around the world and, until 2003, homosexual acts were illegal in 13 states in the US.[8] As Ian Pearson, a British MP has pointed out:[9]

Despite spanning all cultures and countries of the globe, the human rights violations endured by LGBT (lesbians, gay, bisexual and transgender) people are shrouded in silence. The social stigma and prejudice which still surround issues of sexual orientation in many parts of the world mean that many abuses simply go unreported, undocumented and without condemnation.

The UNAIDS secretariat is supposed to provide global leadership for HIV prevention for gay men or 'men who have sex with men', but to date they have been reprehensibly silent. Similarly the evidence shows overwhelmingly that needle-exchange programmes drastically reduce HIV risk for injecting drug users.[10] The results are very encouraging for HIV prevention: a single needle exchange programme in New York led to a 75 per cent decrease in new HIV infections among injecting drug users.[11] Despite such strong evidence, donors have balked at funding these 'harm-reduction' approaches because they are seen to support people doing things that are both illegal and often judged as immoral.

The result of this failure to reach those marginalised groups who are most in need is that HIV prevention reaches less than 9 per cent of gay men, 8 per cent of injecting drug users and less than 20 per cent of sex workers.[12] This is simply not adequate. HIV prevention efforts will never succeed if we can not even manage to provide HIV prevention programmes to those groups which are most vulnerable to HIV infection.

The failure of the UN and individual countries to stand up for the rights of stigmatised groups in society has also been compounded by a shift in the discourse around HIV. This shift was described in Chapter 4: the new focus for HIV responses is now on structural inequalities – exploring the wider factors which make women and poor people vulnerable to HIV infection. The impact of HIV, like other public-health challenges, is closely linked to issues of wider development: those groups who are poor or vulnerable in society will be most at risk of disease and those countries least able to prevent, detect and treat disease will suffer the greatest impact.[13] As such, addressing the wider issues of vulnerability and strengthening underlying systems are now seen to be a key long-term intervention for HIV prevention.

Although we would not argue against taking a structuralist or 'development' approach to HIV prevention, the problem is that, with massive increases in international funding for HIV, too many issue-based groups have been finding a connection – however tenuous – to HIV prevention. As Rasheed points out,

Now HIV is everything and nothing. Everybody finds a connection to HIV, if only to grab a share of the money. Now to solve HIV you have to solve property rights, or violence or income inequality. These things are important in and of themselves but should we be spending HIV prevention money on these things?

The shift to focusing on wider vulnerability factors is important but can also allow the global AIDS community to forget some of the most fundamental issues, such as discussing sex or the needs of highly vulnerable groups such as sex workers or drug users. The shift in focus towards married women – such as Beatrice Were, in Uganda – is important. But it can also exacerbate the problem because these 'good women' (who are seen as innocent victims of male promiscuity) are seen as more deserving than 'bad women' such as sex workers. Indeed, the shift to 'good women' also creates increasingly negative images of men as the spreaders of HIV. This type of analysis risks ignoring the fact that gender relations are not just about the negative behaviours of men but rather the behaviours of men and women in relation to each other.

NO MONEY FOR CONDOMS OR SEX

HIV prevention is failing due to a massive shortage of condoms. The gap between the estimated number of condoms needed for HIV prevention and those supplied in 2005 was 13.1 billion.[14] In Africa, in 2005, only five condoms a year were available for every man between 15 and 59 years old.[15] In 2007, it was estimated that condoms were used in only 9 per cent of risky sex acts worldwide.[16]

Through its international aid for HIV and AIDS, the US government has systematically eroded the reputation of condoms as a form of contraception and as an effective means for HIV prevention. PEPFAR policies and the ensuing push towards abstinence-only approaches have meant that condoms have been reinvented as useful only for high-risk groups. In addition, another piece of insidious American legislation – the Mexico City Policy, more commonly termed the

'Global Gag Rule' – bans American funding of any organisation which provides abortion services, support or counselling.[17]

Population Action International, an American NGO, has been documenting the impact of the Global Gag Rule on the supply of condoms around the world. In their report, *Access Denied*, they describe how many family planning organisations which have refused to stop abortion services have been penalised by having their funding and supplies of condoms cut off. Leading services in 16 poor countries have had their supplies of condoms from the US cut off. For example, in Lesotho, the Lesotho Planned Parenthood Association received 426,000 condoms from the American government between 1998 and 2000 and none from 2000 onwards.[18]

In 2002, the US withdrew $34 million in funding from UNFPA, based on allegations that UNFPA indirectly supported forced abortions in China. As UNFPA is the world's largest condom donor, the repercussions on supply have been huge.[19] Internationally, funding for condoms was $93 million in 2001 and fell to $80 million in 2005.[20] In the year in which the US stopped funding UNFPA, funding for contraceptives fell by 12 per cent.[21]

Following the US withdrawal of funding, several European governments risked damaging US–European relations by making up the shortfall in UNFPA's funding. Although an important temporary stop-gap, this funding has, unfortunately, been tailing off in recent years.[22] The result is a condom shortfall of massive proportions.[23]

In 2005, Uganda needed between 120 and 150 million condoms – but they were given only 30 million, distributed at health clinics. The result was that privately purchased condoms tripled in price from 16 cents to 54 cents for a package of three.[24] The fear tactics used by abstinence-only groups (described in the last chapter) have led to various condom scares in the country. In 2005, more than 30 million quality-approved condoms were impounded in a government warehouse. There were claims that some were defective but this was never substantiated. Beatrice Were recalls:

We had to raise our voices and threaten to sue the government if they did not release them. There were shortages – and even when they did eventually release them, they made no statement to confirm they were safe. The impact on the reputation of condoms was immense. No government representative or policy leader has come out in defence of condoms since then.

This lack of political support for condoms was made clear in a speech by President Museveni in which he called condoms culturally inappropriate for Ugandans and argued that condom distribution encouraged promiscuity among young people.[25]

One UN diplomat who was not afraid to speak his mind was Stephen Lewis, the former UN Special Envoy on AIDS in Africa: 'There is no question that the condom crisis in Uganda is being driven and exacerbated by PEPFAR and by the extreme policies that the administration in the United States is now pursuing.'[26] The Global HIV Prevention Working Group, a panel of leading experts, also criticised the way in which donors are undermining HIV prevention: 'Misallocation of limited resources by donors and affected countries also often occurs as a result of ideological, non-scientific restrictions imposed by donors on how HIV-prevention assistance may be used.'[27]

It is not only the US which has influenced HIV-prevention programmes globally. The UN has also been exporting its own brand of HIV prevention. Curriculum materials on HIV and AIDS look similar across many parts of Africa, Asia and Latin America – despite differences in epidemiology and culture – because they have mostly been designed in North America or Europe.[28] One of the most widespread curricula is called 'life skills' and is based on a package designed by UNICEF – the UN agency responsible for children.

At first, life-skills programmes were uncontroversial. The UNICEF curriculum package did not explicitly discuss sex or explore sexuality directly, thereby reducing potential conflict from the sexually conservative factions that are prominent in many high-prevalence countries. However, through this attempt to make life skills acceptable to governments and communities, the term began to encompass an ever-increasing level of generic skills, leading to the claim that skills as diverse and complex as communicating, listening carefully, income-generating or empathy-building would reduce HIV infection. These claims were (and continue to be) made largely with very little evidential support. In the mental health field and other areas, there is some evidence that life skills have a positive effect on behaviour, but rarely on sexual behaviour, and almost never in developing countries.[29]

Life-skills education is premised on the idea that individuals lack a certain set of life skills. The underlying assumption is that simply teaching about condoms or what people can do to prevent HIV is too mechanistic. Instead, a much broader approach is needed to address the underlying factors that make young people vulnerable.

Although the idea of teaching skills to reduce vulnerability is something we would agree with, the problem is that life skills assumes that complicated human characteristics such as assertiveness or empathy are simple and rational skills which can be taught easily and quickly in a classroom. Concepts such as assertiveness vary from culture to culture, yet the UNICEF curriculum is nearly the same in every country; this leads some critics to accuse the organisation of promoting ideals deriving from Western culture. The validity of generalising across very different types of behaviour, and across different parts of the world, is certainly highly questionable. Even if these skills could be taught, there seems little recognition of the real circumstances faced by the majority of schools in poor countries where teachers are undertrained and overstretched.

There are real difficulties in trying to introduce a particular educational approach into a pre-existing system which is often not receptive to such an approach. Teaching in most classrooms around the world tends to be didactic, non-participatory, inflexible and assessment-driven. In contrast, life-skills education is intended to be participatory and responsive, raising questions rather than providing clear-cut answers, and challenging young people and adults to find new ways of relating to one another. Although more participatory approaches to education should be encouraged, to date not enough thought has gone into how to bridge the gulf between these two different educational processes. Instead, so far, life-skills programmes have been designed that do not fit the current pedagogy in most schools.

Indeed, it is often assumed that teachers will be equipped to teach a radically different curriculum in life skills with a minimal package of in-service training; this is often delivered through a 'cascade approach', in which teachers are trained and then expected to train other teachers. The problem is that at each stage of training the content is diluted and something of the original is lost.

One-off short courses are no substitute for a more comprehensive overhaul of the teacher-training curriculum. But there is little sign of this. Because life-skills education has generally been donor-driven, it has been largely imposed upon systems and schools from the outside. The life-skills curriculum is often not put through the general curriculum planning and review process, and instead is simply 'bolted on' to the main curriculum. The problem here is that school curricula need to be reviewed and adapted holistically, otherwise teachers become overburdened (as is the case in many countries), reducing the potential benefits of any HIV education. Moreover, if the introduction of the life-skills curriculum is viewed as a separate process from that adopted for wider curriculum development, there is likely to be less sense of ownership by curriculum developers and teachers.

To compound these problems, formal education is increasingly assessment-driven, while life skills cannot usually be assessed. Indeed, given its participatory aims, formalising the approach through assessment may give an excessively rigid structure to something that should be flexible.

Given the difficulties in implementing life-skills programmes in schools, the programmes are often given a marginal role within the curriculum, and left to extracurricular activities such as 'anti-AIDS clubs' which, although perhaps more conducive to participatory methodologies, are limited in scope. These are also likely to be non-compulsory and will therefore have reduced coverage.

Despite a dearth of evidence that life-skills education is a successful approach for HIV prevention, the international community has rallied around its implementation in schools. This prioritisation was clearly demonstrated in a special session in 2001 of the United Nations addressing AIDS. Delegates committed themselves to:

By 2005, ensure that at least 90% and by 2010 at least 95% of young men and women aged 15 to 24 have access to the information, education, including peer education and youth-specific HIV education, and services necessary to develop the life skills required to reduce their vulnerability to HIV infection, in full partnership with young persons, parents, educators and health care providers.[30]

The UNICEF curriculum has been taken up across the world. Governments accept these programmes because money is included and governments in poor countries need money. The programme has been popular, partly because it offers an easy route towards being seen to be doing something while avoiding any of the really sensitive issues, such as sex. Any talk of sex or puberty is replaced with vague talk of 'assertiveness' or 'empathy'. Instead of looking at issues of gender and power, the focus is on obtaining an apparently simple set of behavioural skills.[31]

Again the problem lies in people's reluctance to talk about sex. Almost everyone feels awkward or embarrassed talking about sex at some point or other, or in some way or another. But the reality is that the vast majority of HIV infections are transmitted through sex and therefore HIV prevention in schools cannot work without reference to sex. Children need to have good-quality sex education which frankly discusses issues of growing up, family planning and prevention of sexually transmitted infections. This is now a matter of life or death. If young people are infected because they have not been taught how to prevent infection, there should be outrage. It is time to challenge the cosy consensus that HIV education can be achieved without any mention of sex and sexual relationships. The conspiracy of silence is wide and deep and the power dynamics that sustain that silence are complex – but they need to be exposed.

DEADLY INERTIA

In order to start breaking the silence around HIV and sex, in 2005 we conducted a survey on behalf of the Global Campaign for Education (GCE) into how well national governments in 18 countries were providing HIV and AIDS education in schools.[32] The shocking finding was that international donor policies were not necessarily helping governments but were inadvertently causing a host of problems which hampered the response.

Of the 18 countries, only two had a coherent education-sector AIDS strategy that was actually being implemented. In the Asian and Latin American countries, there was no policy response from ministries of education, firstly because HIV was seen as the responsibility of ministries of health and secondly because HIV was not deemed a serious problem.

In Africa, ministries of education made varying levels of progress in developing and implementing an HIV strategy for the education sector. In most countries, the development of a specific HIV and AIDS strategy for the education sector had been funded by international donors. Typically, this meant that a group of stakeholders came together and wrote a paper on what the education sector should do to respond to HIV and AIDS. However, because these specific plans were donor-driven, they were often outside the normal planning process of ministries and therefore carried very little weight politically.

While international donors ask governments to sign various pledges, communiqués or plans, the governments concerned know that they will rarely be held accountable. Often these plans or commitments are so grandiose or else so general that they are never going to be feasible to implement at a realistic scale, given how poor some of these countries are. The lack of serious commitment to these plans is evidenced by the GCE research which showed that the vast majority of the education and HIV proposals had not even been costed: rather than creating a feasible plan, they were more like a wish list with little chance of being implemented.

The GCE report found that many donors have encouraged ministries of education to employ an HIV and AIDS coordinator. While based within national government, these coordinators are mostly funded by donors and so tend to be isolated from the core working of the ministry and lacking in political power. In many cases, the donors had funded the salary of the coordinator but provided no budget for activities, so that this person was operating without any money.[33]

In fact, most of the HIV response in ministries of education is donor-funded. In a rush to get HIV education on the agenda as quickly as possible, donors have bypassed the existing processes and procedures for introducing new materials and have produced their own resource materials. As with life skills, donor-driven curricula are not developed through the core curriculum design processes and since the general curriculum is already overloaded in most countries, this means that HIV and AIDS modules tend to be ignored or neglected.

The result in schools is that HIV education is not taken seriously, either by teachers or by ministry officials. Real ownership is low. What is more, the alarm raised by Europeans and North Americans over the AIDS crisis has sometimes been interpreted as part of a colonial legacy and as racist, especially against Africans.

AIDS IMPOSED ON AFRICA

Chapter 4 began to tell the story of South Africa and the controversial stand of its president, Thabo Mbeki. Mbeki has been vilified by the international donor community for being an AIDS sceptic and for not having done enough to prevent one of the worst HIV epidemics in the world.[34]

Over the years, Mbeki has consistently questioned the basic science underlying our understanding of HIV and AIDS and has stalled in providing treatment or prevention services to those in need.[35] This scepticism has undoubtedly cost thousands of South Africans their lives. Despite this, however, it is important to understand where Mbeki is coming from, because it connects to many of the obstacles that are experienced elsewhere as North American and European donors play an increasingly dominant role in driving the response to HIV and AIDS.

As an articulate and highly educated man, Mbeki's attitude towards HIV and AIDS surprised many. However, as a champion of the African Renaissance, one can begin to understand why he raised concerns on seeing Europeans and North Americans demanding action from his government on HIV and African 'promiscuity'. Acutely aware of the colonial literature on black sexuality, he asked for the space to allow Africans to find African solutions to their own problems. At a public speech to university students in 2001, Mbeki stated:

Convinced that we are but natural-born, promiscuous carriers of germs, unique in the world, they proclaim that our continent is doomed to an inevitable mortal end because of our unconquerable devotion to the sin of lust.[36]

An article from the *New Yorker* in 2003 summarised this perspective.

The politics of AIDS had long been racially charged. Conspiracy theories had circulated all over Africa, and even among some African-Americans, suggesting that AIDS was part of a plot to wipe out blacks.[37]

Given South Africa's history of apartheid, these fears were not entirely unsubstantiated. The apartheid government was accused of sponsoring a clandestine germ-warfare programme that targeted officials of the opposition party, the ANC. Openly racist comments about HIV and AIDS in South Africa are still part of deeply held stereotypes of African sexuality as violent and uncontrolled.[38] When the AIDS crisis started, a white politician even said publicly: 'If AIDS stops black population growth, it would be like Father Christmas.'[39]

Mbeki's stance is less one of denial than one of active defiance against the aid industry and AIDS experts from Europe and North America. Observers suggest that Mbeki still views AIDS as a new colonial looting of Africa, exploiting deeply rooted racist stereotypes of black sexuality.[40] From this conspiratorial viewpoint, the international pharmaceutical companies have constructed the myth of AIDS as a generic term for multiple illnesses (which are diseases of poverty) so that ARVs can be sold – not as cures but as permanent treatments from which the companies can draw reliable annual profits in perpetuity. The resistance shown by these companies to the use of cheap generic drugs is taken as evidence that their only interest is profit – and the companies now have academics, donors and UN agencies promoting their agenda.[41]

This view is clearly and undoubtedly mistaken but in the context of South Africa's history, one can understand how it emerged.

Furthermore, the vilification of Mbeki by the Western media for his AIDS 'denialism' has probably reinforced the impression by many Africans of there being a conspiracy.

The significance of this wider history and political climate is considerable. HIV and AIDS are pushed up the political agenda by European and North American donors. For some Africans, it seems like a new colonial project: saving poor Africans from themselves. But there is so much history of white people constructing racist images of black sexuality that it is easy to understand why there has been resistance against European or American demands that South Africans talk about sex and death in their classrooms. The negative consequence of this is a lack of ownership over HIV prevention efforts.

Although international donors have laudably prioritised funding for HIV over the last five years, one unfortunately inadvertent consequence has been the perception that this benevolent assistance is an implicit criticism of Africa, Africa's ability to deal with her own issues and African promiscuity.

The more governments feel imposed upon the more they might end up resisting. There is no doubt that too many HIV prevention efforts have been donor-led or donor-imported, creating little bubbles of activity rather than an integrated response. The legacy of colonialism and the politics of aid have undermined the potential of HIV prevention to reach the most vulnerable groups – and have undermined the potential of schools to provide open and accurate discussions on HIV and sex.

9
The Power of Money

As the world finally woke up to the global crisis in HIV and AIDS, unprecedented amounts of funding became available. Between 1996 and 2005, the annual funding for HIV and AIDS in low- and middle-income countries grew from an estimated $300 million to $8.3 billion.[1] Global efforts to prevent HIV have mostly been funded through the international aid community. However, fundamental problems in the way aid is provided to poor countries undermine the ability to respond to the HIV epidemic.

GIVING WITH ONE HAND

The biggest problems with aid are political ones. Overwhelmingly, aid is driven by geopolitical and commercial objectives rather than by efforts to prevent HIV. The overt objectives of international aid are to reduce poverty yet a simple analysis of which countries receive official aid shows that this is not the case. Only 40 per cent of aid goes to low-income countries, despite their accounting for more than three quarters of all people living in poverty.[2] The European Commission gives almost three quarters of its aid budget to middle-income countries. Shockingly, there are no sub-Saharan African countries in their list of top ten aid recipients.

So what actually influences which countries receive the most money? ActionAid recently conducted a report which tracked aid money and found that since the 11 September 2001 attacks on the US, aid has become increasingly politicised, with aid allocations favouring strategic allies in the 'war on terror'.[3]

Just over $2.5 billion in international aid goes to funding basic education. Less than a third of this goes to sub-Saharan Africa, where the need is greatest. The commitments made in international conferences on aid are simply not being met in practice. Of the $23 billion spent on aid by the US government, less than $0.5 billion goes to support basic education.[4]

Even if aid targets the countries which are most in need, 40 per cent of the money continues to be officially tied. This means that countries receiving the aid have to buy certain goods or services from the donor country. In effect a large part of the aid so generously given ends up benefiting the rich country rather than the poor country. It is estimated that the value of aid would be boosted by $5–7 billion each year if aid were untied.[5]

Aid for HIV and AIDS particularly suffers from being tied to buying certain products. Despite the increasing availability of generic treatments for HIV, PEPFAR funding stipulates that the money can only be used to buy branded drugs. This favours the large pharmaceutical companies (many of which are American) but ultimately means that fewer people are accessing treatment.[6]

There are similar problems with aid for HIV and education being tied to 'technical assistance' provided by the donor country. In 2003, $18 billion of donor money, or more than a quarter of total aid, was allocated to technical assistance. This is supposed to provide expert support to poor countries. The problem is that it is often heavily tied to buying in expertise from consultants from the donor country. Donor governments such as the UK or the US are more likely to hire experts from their own country rather than from developing countries.[7]

In Africa alone, donors employ an estimated 100,000 technical experts.[8] In Cambodia, the amount of money spent on international consultants could have paid for a year's salary for 160,000 civil servants. Instead, donor money was spent on international consultants who charged up to 200 times more than a local person would charge.[9] Would it not make more sense to invest in local expertise and human capacity, which is cheaper, more relevant and more sustainable in the long-term?

Similar problems exist with technical assistance for education. A recent review of technical assistance to education projects in Ghana exposed the contradictions.[10] While foreign technical experts are supposed to train local counterparts, this rarely happens; the relationship between consultants and local staff is often patronising; no consultant ever goes unpaid for having failed to deliver the terms of their contract; there is little coordination between consultants and the core ministry departments they are supposed to work with; there is no transparency about consultants' terms of reference or fees; and there is no institutional learning generated. Most consultants' reports were also found to have been written in the language of the donor (whether Japanese or German) and rarely translated. In the education sector in Ghana alone, 18 key posts were funded by donors who were paying over the going rate for staff to support their own programmatic agendas, undermining and distorting local pay structures and the management systems of ministries.

Not only is funding for HIV prevention often tied to buying certain services or products, it is also tied to certain models of HIV prevention. As has been argued throughout this book, models such as abstinence-only or life skills are exported to countries with little consideration of local realities.

Models for HIV education are developed in Europe or North America and are often of little value for Africa and Asia. They include all the right things: psycho-social support for children, making schools into caring environments, putting in place workplace policies for teachers. But too often these are not realistic or even relevant to local circumstances.. Even schools in the US or Europe would struggle to apply them, let alone resource-poor schools in Africa. But as the funding is tied to particular models of prevention, governments take them up even where there is little hope of ever implementing them.

WASTED AID AND THE DEMOCRATIC DEFICIT

Although aid is supposed to help poor countries tackle HIV and get children into school, it inadvertently imposes additional burdens for governments of recipient countries. In exchange for aid, governments are expected to meet a whole host of requirements, ranging from issues around disbursement and procurement, to reporting and monitoring. As donors do not usually pool their funding, governments will have multiple reporting responsibilities which will differ for each donor. Far too much time – which should be spent on implementing programmes – is wasted on fulfilling the reporting requirements of donor governments. A typical African country submits 10,000 reports each year, and hosts more than 1,000 visits from donor countries.[11] In far too many cases, this is a damaging and unproductive drain on local resources.

Countries jump through so many hoops to get the aid money that they lose sight of the actual delivery. They do more to keep the donors happy and to report to the donors than they do to report or account to their own people. For individual officials, building a relationship with and satisfying the donor is a good career move that can lead to well-paid jobs and consultancies in the future. Many of the most capable government staff end up being taken on by donors and are then given jobs to advise the government that they have just left. The problem is that these people would be better off implementing programmes in government than merely offering advice through inefficient technical assistance.

A lack of coordination between donors and other development partners also undermines HIV prevention because young people receive conflicting and confusing messages. Some NGOs teach about abstinence-only and refuse to discuss condoms while other organisations will teach about condoms.[12] PEPFAR even includes a 'conscience clause' which stipulates that religious groups do not have to teach about all forms of HIV prevention if the organisation has a religious or moral objection.[13] All too often, governments are not in control of what is being taught in the name of HIV prevention in their schools.

Not only is aid wasted but it is often spent on providing parallel services which undermine government efforts. In Uganda, Beatrice Were recalls that a few years ago there was consensus on how an effective response to HIV and AIDS would depend on building good-quality public-health provision:

We said we would improve the Ugandan health system – we would strengthen public health – but in practice the money has come in to create parallel systems, undermining the government provision and splintering the response. Countless small organisations are directly funded – and they have no accountability to the Ministry of Health. Rather, they all account to USAID.

Yes, PEPFAR reaches more with treatment – but without a strong health system, that intervention is not sustainable. Without the right human resources across the country you can't reach out. I would rather have less money now but do what is right and respect public health and human rights.

In Zambia, locals complain that PEPFAR is funding American organisations to provide treatment and HIV prevention in communities, eroding the progress made by government. These US-funded programmes pay much higher salaries than the local NGOs so expertise is being drained away from home-grown sustainable programmes to PEPFAR-funded programmes which may end at any time.[14]

Even if aid is given for HIV prevention, governments are often not able to use it to develop the underlying health and education infrastructure because the money is too unpredictable and short-term. Most donors are unable to make commitments for more than three years. Moreover, even once committed, aid often arrives late.

For example, one study by Oxfam entitled *Paying the Price* found that 86 per cent of aid from the European Commission arrives late.[15] Unreliable aid both undermines long-term planning and creates financial uncertainty for governments.

As a result of this unpredictability, aid money is rarely spent on the things that are most urgently needed. The biggest need is to invest in training and employing more frontline staff – but the aid money doesn't do this. Most aid money comes for short-term projects that take for granted that teachers, doctors and nurses are already there: in most places, however, they simply are not there in adequate numbers to ensure quality delivery of services, let alone take on new responsibilities because of HIV.

There is a growing consensus, including among some more progressive donors, that aid money should no longer come in two- or three-year cycles, because nobody can plan effectively in this short-term way. The UK government, through the Department for International Development (DfID) has encouraged governments to develop ten-year plans for education, though it has yet to resolve how they can deliver such long-term aid in practice. The European Commission is talking about five-year contracts – but again this approach exists so far only on paper.

If progress is made on increasing the predictability of aid then recipient governments could start making the longer-term changes which are urgently needed to respond to the interconnected challenges of HIV and education. Governments would be able to support the real priorities; such as the training and employment of more teachers, doctors and nurses. They would also be able to build up the underlying infrastructure of their societies, rather than struggling to layer endless new programmes and projects on a crumbling base.

The politics of the aid industry mean that most projects are designed on desks far away and then imposed on recipient countries. The programmes can define the fundamental direction of reforms to health or education yet they mostly end up being negotiated directly between the relevant ministry and the donor, bypassing the domestic political process and not being answerable to the electorate. In democratic countries, one would expect major policy decisions to be made by elected members of government through a democratic process of debate and consensus. With aid, this decision-making process is often bypassed and, once again, governments end up being more accountable to the aid industry than to their own citizens.[16]

Some progress is being made. The reform of the UN is leading to greater coordination in some countries, with all UN agencies developing a shared work-plan and budget. There is a move towards giving Direct Budget Support to governments, enabling them to receive core funding for their government budget if they have an effective plan to reduce poverty and achieve basic development goals. This is the focus of extensive international debate but to date relatively little aid actually ends up going through this route.

THE FUTURE OF AID

Given all the inefficiencies and politics of international aid, what is the future for this multi-billion dollar industry? There are enough good exceptions to suggest that with significant reform, aid can lead to more positive outcomes. Aid can be used effectively to improve school enrolment and prevent HIV. In Uganda, for example, donors have been providing both budget support and debt relief to fund poverty-reduction programmes. This aid has been untied, reasonably predictable and well coordinated. As a result, it has helped to fund a huge expansion in primary school enrolment, from 3 million children in 1997 to almost 8 million by 2003.[17] Despite all the problems and inefficiencies, international aid (in combination with government investment) has contributed to a doubling of school enrolments and a halving of infant mortality.[18]

This impact could be even greater if donors better harmonised their efforts with the national plans of recipient governments. This is the intention behind the Paris Declaration,[19] endorsed in March 2005 by more than 100 ministers, heads of development agencies and other senior officials at a meeting hosted by the OECD's Development Assistance Committee.[20] This declaration offers a practical, action-oriented road map to improve the quality and harmonisation of aid.

Specific attempts to coordinate international aid for education have focused on the setting up of the Fast Track Initiative (FTI).[21] Set up in 2002, this is based on the idea that each country should come up with a single education sector plan. This plan is then reviewed against some basic benchmarks and, if approved, a pooled group of international donor agencies, including the UN agencies and bilaterals, would then pledge to coordinate their efforts to fund the plan. One country, one plan. This is a much better set-up than currently prevails with funding for HIV and AIDS. Many governments across Africa, Asia and Latin America have responded by developing comprehensive education plans, and many of these have now been endorsed by the FTI.

Unfortunately the donor countries have failed to come up with sufficient money to fund the plans. Some increase in aid for education was evident initially, with aid to education rising to about $4.4 billion a year in 2004, but it has since slumped back to $3 billion a year. In 2007, the FTI had a funding shortfall of US$500 million for delivering funding for the 32 country plans it had already approved.[22]

Despite these problems, the FTI has certainly improved coordination between donors. The wasteful duplication of the past has been reduced and funds channelled through the FTI are not subject to the same tied-aid constraints of so much aid to education. In many respects, the FTI remains a positive example. The focus is on supporting and strengthening an in-country process rather than taking decisions in Washington or in Europe. Moreover, increasing attention is being given to the role of coordinated consultation between national governments and their citizens, through the involvement of broad-based civil society coalitions. The overall governance structure of the FTI now includes both developing-country representatives and the Global Campaign for Education, ensuring greater transparency than in the past.

Similarly laudable efforts have been made to coordinate aid funding for HIV and AIDS. In 2002, the same year in which the FTI was founded for education, an ambitious multilateral mechanism was set up called the Global Fund to Fight AIDS, Tuberculosis and Malaria. The Global Fund is an international public-private initiative launched to help raise the resources needed to effectively combat HIV and AIDS globally. It is designed to overcome some of the criticisms about aid money being wasted and programmes being imposed rather than adequately owned by countries. As with the FTI, the Global Fund is structured to ensure country ownership of programmes, with a strong civil society element. The process of deciding which countries should receive grants involves a wide range of technical experts and prevents donor countries from attaching their own conditions to the aid granted.

The Global Fund states that 'the highest priority will be given to proposals from countries and regions with the greatest need, based on the highest burden of disease and the least ability to bring the required additional financial resources to address these health problems'.[23] The Global Fund is broadly democratic with donor and developing country governments each occupying seven seats on the board. The board also includes two NGOs and two private-sector donors. The NGO seats include one representative of NGOs from the South and one representative of NGOs from the North.

Being outside the UN system, the Global Fund is able to minimise bureaucratic delays and maximise flexibility. Proposals have been screened, reviewed and approved at a rapid pace.[24] However, on the flip side, there has been competition between the UNAIDS Secretariat and the Global Fund and relations between the two have not been as collaborative as one would have hoped for.[25]

The Global Fund is one of the few funding mechanisms that truly allow countries to decide their own priorities. The Global Fund is designed to support proven interventions as identified by the recipient countries, rather than by donors. Recipient countries are usually far better positioned to know what types of interventions are needed, feasible and culturally appropriate.

The Global Fund is an innovative and successful mechanism for coordinating aid for HIV prevention. In June 2007, the leaders of the world's richest countries (the G8) agreed that funding for the Global Fund should be increased six-fold by 2010.[26] However, these commitments often have not translated into actual increases in funding. At the most recent Global Fund meeting in 2007, only $9.7 billion was pledged out of the $18 billion which was needed for programmes from 2008 to 2010. This is significantly more money than the FTI has managed to mobilise for education but still far less than what is needed.

The problem is that donor governments are still hesitant to give their money through multilateral structures such as the Global Fund or the FTI. Instead, they prefer to fund their own programmes bilaterally. The US is an obvious example: to date, the American government has given only $2.5 billion to the Global Fund while simultaneously pledging $15 billion through PEPFAR,[27] of which $14 billion is for direct bilateral aid.[28] As has been argued numerous times in this book, PEPFAR is aid at its worst – tied to the purchasing of certain models of HIV prevention and certain products, and in many cases undermining government provision of basic services.

Even when aid for HIV has been made available, far too little has been spent on HIV prevention.[29] The Global HIV Prevention Working Group cites a number of reasons why HIV prevention has not received the level of funding needed. One reason is that the time-frame for HIV prevention is longer than the term of a political leader, which creates a political disincentive for action. Politicians are under pressure to produce results and success in HIV prevention is an absence of HIV, which is not a very achievable result.[30] For HIV prevention to work, programmes must be complex and require frank discussions about sensitive issues – something which politicians try to ignore.

CONTRADICTING COMMITMENTS

Even if all the money that has been promised in aid for education and for HIV was suddenly made available, fundamental contradictions in the architecture of international finance would still prevent large amounts of it from being spent where it is needed.

The International Monetary Fund (IMF) plays a highly important role in rating the economic competence of countries. It provides credit ratings on all countries and these ratings are used by businesses when making decisions about whether to invest or not. The IMF uses this power to suggest macroeconomic changes that it thinks will reduce macroeconomic instability, which is necessary for reducing poverty in the country. Sometimes, the IMF advice comes as an absolute binding condition on a loan. But even where it does not provide loans, the IMF's hegemonic control over macroeconomic policies means that no government can afford to ignore it altogether.

The problem, as Rick Rowden, an ActionAid policy analyst, discovered, was that the macroeconomic policies advocated and imposed by the IMF have terrible effects on basic services such as education and health. Effectively, they undermine attempts to prevent HIV or achieve any of the international development targets.

Why are more than 4,000 trained nurses and thousands of other health workers in Kenya sitting unemployed when they should be working to combat the HIV/AIDS emergency in their country? It all comes down to the IMF and macroeconomics [and] this is the point where most people switch off.

UNESCO estimates that 18 million new teachers are needed globally between now and 2015 in order to get all children into school in acceptable class sizes. At least 2.4 million new teachers will be needed in sub-Saharan Africa.[31] The World Health Organisation (WHO) estimates that there is currently a global shortage of 4.3 million health workers, especially in sub-Saharan Africa and south Asia.[32] But in many of these countries, the IMF imposes a 'public-sector wage-bill cap'. This imposes limits on how much the government is allowed to spend on the salaries of public-sector workers; this leads to Rick's example of the thousands of unemployed Kenyan nurses despite an urgent need for their services.

The IMF argues that wage-bill caps are essential to cut back bloated government bureaucracies, but teachers and health workers comprise the largest group of people on government payrolls. In practice, when the public-sector wage bill is squeezed, it is frontline workers in essential services that are usually the main victims.[33]

In many other countries, Rick found that the IMF avoids directly imposing a wage cap. Instead the IMF requires countries to focus all their attention on keeping fiscal deficit levels very low, and keeping inflation down to less than 5 per cent. In order to meet these main IMF loan conditions, ministries of finance have little choice but to freeze salaries and block the recruitment of more teachers and medical staff. Any growth in public-sector spending on salaries could increase the deficit or the amount of liquidity in the money supply and thus push up inflation, according to the IMF.[34]

This all sounds very similar to the 'structural adjustment' of the 1980s. Indeed, it is exactly the same policy but in new packaging. Today, these policies aim to ensure stability and promote poverty reduction but the overly restrictive macroeconomic conditions imposed on countries have the effect of reducing spending on education and health – two important drivers for development.

Indeed, ministries of education are rarely, if ever, consulted by the IMF about these economic targets. The dialogue happens privately between the IMF and finance ministries.[35] Despite compelling evidence that education is one of the soundest long-term economic investments a country can make, the IMF regards spending on education as 'pure consumption' rather than as a 'productive investment'.[36]

The impact of these IMF constraints on wage bills is very evident in Kenya. In 2003, the government abolished school fees and implemented a policy of free primary education. More than a million children enrolled in school for the first time. However, in 1998 the IMF had set a cap on the number of teachers the government of Kenya could employ, limiting the number at 235,000 teachers. Even when enrolment rose dramatically, the cap was not lifted and the government was unable to recruit more teachers.[37] Class sizes rose dramatically and in rural schools the pupil–teacher ratios reached excessive levels, with teachers often facing classrooms of more than 100 children. The result was that the quality of education plummeted. The ironic thing was that there were unemployed teachers available and ready to teach. The government just was not allowed to employ them.

By 2007, there were 2 million more children in school than in 2003 and after much lobbying to demand more teachers just 4,000 new teachers have been recruited. That works out as one new teacher for every 500 new children.[38]

One way that governments have circumnavigated the constraints on teacher salaries is to stop employing newly trained teachers. Instead, they start employing less qualified teachers. Non-professional teachers can usually be recruited on a third of a qualified teacher's salary – and as there is no need to pay for training other savings are also made.[39] Another simple cost-saving measure is to issue ten-month contracts so that salaries do not have to be paid during the long summer holidays. As noted in Chapter 3, there is little hope of such teachers dealing effectively with HIV if they have not even received basic training – and they have no idea whether they will have a job next year.

Precisely the same constraints and pressures are felt by the health system. After teachers, the second largest group of workers on many government payrolls is usually health workers – doctors and nurses. A report in 2007 by the US NGO, Center for Global Development[40] showed how wage-bill caps in 17 of the 42 IMF programmes they studied included wage-bill ceilings. The author of this report, David Goldsborough, observed:[41]

The effect of [IMF] programmes on health spending is controversial. Those who have worked hard in the past decade to mobilise unprecedented levels of funding and attention for health programs in developing countries have contended that the IMF's approach to macroeconomic management has constrained effective use of donor funds and therefore weakened efforts to improve health conditions in countries that are most heavily burdened by disease.

The report also found that there was a striking lack of connection between macroeconomic and health-sector policy-making: 'Key fiscal decisions are taken with little understanding of potential consequences for the health sector, and health ministries typically cannot make an effective case for increased budgetary priority.'

Even UNAIDS has now recognised the extent to which IMF policies are undermining the response to the AIDS crisis. Peter Piot, the executive director, recently stated: 'When I hear that countries are choosing to comply with the budget ceilings at the expense of adequately funding AIDS programs, it strikes me that someone isn't looking hard enough for sound alternatives.'[42]

In addition to public-sector wage caps, some countries are hesitant to accept aid money in case it disrupts agreements with the IMF. In 2002–03, the government of Uganda nearly rejected $52 million in funding for HIV in order to please the IMF.[43] One of the main reasons was that the Ugandan government had already set the budget ceiling for the health sector for the following three years and this additional aid money would cause them to go over the agreed limit and thus jeopardise their credit rating with the IMF.

The donors and press were vocal in criticising the Ugandan government for rejecting money for HIV but the Ministry of Finance insisted that they had agreed with the IMF that there would be no further increases in the health budget. In an attempt to find a solution, the government suggested cutting $52 million from other parts of the health budget to accommodate the additional aid money. This caused even greater outrage: the aim was to give additional money for HIV, not to take money away from somewhere else. After pressure from activists like Rick Rowden, the government finally relented to public campaigning and broke their arrangement with the IMF.[44]

These types of pressures exist in nearly all impoverished countries that are seeking to respond to the crisis in HIV and education. Indeed, the whole aid industry risks being undermined by the IMF's policies. One problem is that the IMF routinely underestimates how much aid a country is likely to receive from donors and thus creates conditions in which countries are unable to absorb more aid if it does come.[45] The unintended impact of this is far-reaching. Countries can end up developing and adopting less ambitious plans to reduce poverty because they are advised that too much aid will destabilise their macroeconomic stability.

An additional problem was exposed by the IMF's own Independent Evaluation Office (IEO) in their report in 2007.[46] This evaluation revealed that during the period from 2005 to 2007, the IMF advised countries with inflation rates higher than 5 per cent only to spend 15 per cent of anticipated increases in additional funding. The rest of the aid money (85 per cent) was to be used to build up currency reserves and pay off domestic debt. In countries where inflation was under 5 per cent, the IMF advised them to put 21 per cent of the aid into their reserves. In practice, this meant that many of the poorest countries were unable to spend their aid on what it had been programmed for, having instead to pay off debt and build up reserves in case of economic instability. This is scandalous and it is difficult to understand why donors have not complained that their money has been misspent. If a government of a poor country had decided unilaterally to use aid for paying off debts, there would have been public outrage, both from the public in that country and donor countries.

Rick argues that the IMF's policy on wage ceilings is a symptom of a deeper problem:

Even if the IMF were to eliminate wage-bill ceilings completely, the overall problems would still persist because of the unnecessarily restrictive fiscal and monetary policies required of countries by the IMF. They set strict targets for deficit-reduction and inflation-reduction – which means countries end up with smaller national budgets than they could otherwise have. There are alternative policies that could be followed … but the IMF doesn't advise countries on these alternatives. They tend to offer just one recipe – an extremely restrictive one – for everyone, regardless of country context.

It is assumed by the IMF that countries must keep inflation under 5 per cent if they are to be stable and capable of investing in development. Clearly it is important to keep levels of inflation low but there are other considerations which countries should take account of.[47]

In the 1980s, when several countries faced hyperinflation crises, there was a strong rationale for placing inflation at the absolute centre of concerns. However, continuing with such an approach today is at odds with the new imperative to greatly scaled-up public investment, especially spending on education and health. Most countries now have low or modest inflation and only extreme examples stand out as exceptions, such as Zimbabwe. It is much less clear whether keeping inflation under 5 per cent today should be the non-negotiable concern when the most economically productive citizens of many countries are dying on an unprecedented scale because of AIDS.[48]

There are those in the IMF who acknowledge the problem. For example, Andy Berg of the IMF admits, 'reducing inflation from high levels can carry real costs in the short run'.[49] These real costs include lower growth rates and insufficient funding to employ urgently needed teachers and doctors. There is a term for this in the economic literature which is almost visibly appropriate. It is the 'sacrifice ratio'.

As Rick explains:

For the IMF it is a cold calculation: to achieve their ideological short-term goals on monetary policy, health and education investments in the long-term have to be sacrificed. The IMF have never asked poor people whether they would prefer to keep inflation at 5 per cent and have no school for their children ... or whether perhaps they would prefer inflation to be running at 10 per cent but have access to decent-quality education and basic health provision. Of course the trade off is not quite so simple – but there is a trade off here and what is clear is that the governments of poor countries (let alone poor people themselves) are never given a choice.

Why aren't countries demanding a debate about these trade-offs between targets in inflation and development? Rick conducted interviews with officials in the central banks, finance ministries and health and education ministries in Bangladesh, Ghana, Malawi, Uganda and Zambia.[50]

We revealed two difficulties. Firstly, most central bank and finance ministry officials have internalised IMF economics and do not or will not acknowledge the possibility of more expansionary fiscal and monetary policies. Secondly, health and education ministry officials are locked out of the process; the health ministry official in Malawi said that the ministry is given a spending ceiling, but how the ceiling is arrived at is not known.

So, what can be done? However much the IMF is challenged in Washington and however many reports are written, it will not be enough. The target instead has to be with national governments. Ministers of finance in the G8 countries dominate the IMF Board. Surely they should be concerned that their taxpayers' money, which they are sending to poor countries through their aid budgets, is not being used effectively because of conditions imposed by the IMF? Citizens in these countries – taxpayers – certainly should protest. But pressure is also needed on the governments of poor countries so that citizens can demand that their ministries of finance are transparent about their dealings with the IMF and stand up to the IMF when conditions are being imposed which undermine national development. To do this, the economic knowledge and capacity of civil-society activists need to be developed so that they can ask the right questions of their finance ministers and central banks and demand open debate of the options in national parliaments and in the media. As Rick observes:

Ultimately these people can be held democratically accountable in most countries – if citizens, parliaments, national media understand that there are alternatives. We need people to come together – education, health and HIV campaigners, NGOs, social movements and unions – together we can build a formidable force. We need a new abstinence movement – a movement that urges governments to 'just say no' when the IMF comes to town.

In part due to exactly the type of political lobbying and activism described above, the IMF is beginning to reform under pressure. During 2007, there were some dramatic breakthroughs. Following the IEO's evaluation and reports from ActionAid and the Center for Global Development, the IMF committed itself to moving away from the use of public sector wage-bill caps as a routine policy. The IMF is now recommending that this policy is kept in reserve for situations of extreme macroeconomic instability, but accepts that it can no longer use them so widely.[51] This is clearly a cause for some celebration and highlights the important role that political activism and civil society can play. But equally, it is important to recognise that this is just a first step.

10
Concluding Remarks

The last 30 years have witnessed a global crisis in AIDS and education. Nearly 33 million people[1] are thought to be infected with a virus for which there is still no cure and still no vaccine.

One of the most frustrating aspects of this crisis is that we know how to prevent HIV infection and yet we are failing to take the action needed. For most people, HIV is transmitted through sexual intercourse and, like other sexually transmitted infections, there are a number of strategies to minimise the risk of becoming infected.

Put like this, the problem and solution seem straightforward. Why then, have efforts at HIV prevention failed so dismally? This book has attempted to answer this question by looking at the underlying politics, which have created an epidemic of prejudice, pitted ideology against science and created an aid system that is inefficient and self-serving.

The epidemic of prejudice is best understood through the human stories told by Teo, Somchai and others. These people, from different parts of the world, have all experienced the terrible effects of the stigma that HIV carries. People fear the unknown and, at first, people feared an unknown virus that killed. A similar thing happened with cancer: people who were diagnosed with cancer 20 years ago often recount stories of rejection. The difference is that today, although cancer is an illness that is still feared, cancer patients are viewed as victims. With HIV, blame and rejection continue to dominate. It is proving more difficult to break the stigma related to HIV than cancer because HIV is associated with sex – and sex is surrounded by taboos and moral judgments.

There are some groups in society who are more likely to get HIV because of their sexual practices: gay men and sex workers. These two groups deviate from the commonly expected sexual norm of 'monogamous heterosexual relationships' and thus are already socially marginalised. With their particular vulnerability to HIV infection, this marginalisation has only deepened.

Governments often shy away from supporting these groups because they are so stigmatised against by much of society. Indeed, widely held ideological beliefs lead people to ignore the fact that such groups exist. Arguing that these groups exist and need support is often difficult.

In this context, the marginalised groups have to organise for themselves, as the sex workers have in Brazil and gay men did in the US. The programmes they design for themselves have been among the most effective. They know that to prevent HIV there is no point in telling sex workers to stop selling sex and there is no point in telling gay men not to have homosexual sex.

In Africa, it is now becoming clear that women are more vulnerable than men to HIV. Three-quarters of new infections among young people are among women.[2] It is also clear that those with less education are much more likely to be infected – and those who are rich can afford treatment and are able to conceal their status. This is making HIV progressively into a disease of poor African women, adding another dimension to the multiple forms of marginalisation from which they already suffer. Prejudice about HIV thus feeds on other prejudices – and becomes harder to challenge.

Poor African women have little political voice and there are few examples of them organising for themselves. Few governments will give priority to such a group and very little of the funding now available finds its way to them. Programmes which do target women or marginalised groups are rarely designed with the meaningful involvement of the marginalised groups or people living with HIV in mind. This is the politics of prejudice. In response, solidarity needs to be fostered between people living with HIV so that they can, collectively, join forces and speak out. HIV prevention needs to become political.

Actively involving women does not mean that programmes need to be targeted only at women. Indeed, targeting programmes just at the most vulnerable groups can reinforce prejudice in wider society. Besides, although rates of HIV infection amongst women are higher, change will not be achieved without addressing the attitudes and behaviour of men. This indeed, is perhaps the biggest challenge. As Beatrice noted in Chapter 7, she abstained until marriage and was faithful in marriage, but this did not protect her from getting HIV.

In countries where the epidemic has spread to the general population, it is important that education programmes make it clear that everyone is at risk, not just specially labelled groups. But while programmes should be designed to reach out to everyone, they should be developed with the active involvement of the most affected groups, especially people living with HIV and AIDS. The example of Kindlimuka in Mozambique bears this out – and the challenge is to apply such programmes on a wider scale.

Indeed, there are many examples of effective programmes that have challenged prejudice, raised awareness and offered practical advice. Soul Buddyz in South Africa has done this on an impressive scale through its 'edutainment' programmes. But success does not depend solely on big organisations. Individuals can also make a difference, like Ms Daopahai, the teacher in Thailand who has transformed the life chances of her student, Kwanjai. Schools can play a pivotal role providing children with emotional support, especially when their parents are ill or dying, as we have seen in Swaziland – with their multiple circles of support. Adult-learning programmes like STAR are also making a real difference.

Although education efforts need to go beyond schools, the classroom has a central role in HIV prevention efforts simply because it is one of the most effective ways of reaching large numbers of young people who – by and large – are not yet infected with HIV. Schools must rise to the challenge of preparing children to navigate their way in a world with HIV. Each new year-group in a school is a new opportunity for preventing HIV – they could be the first HIV-free generation. As such, each year that children leave school without the knowledge, attitudes and behaviour that could protect them from HIV presents a huge missed opportunity.

But it is not easy for schools and teachers to launch the comprehensive HIV and AIDS education programmes that are needed. The reality is that in many countries, teachers are overworked, underpaid, poorly trained and not prepared to teach about sex or HIV. Educational problems are compounded by the large number of children who have been orphaned or affected by HIV and AIDS, and who might not be able to afford to go to school or else will need additional support.

Despite these real and serious constraints facing schools in poor countries, HIV prevention programmes in schools can succeed. There are some common threads that run through HIV prevention programmes that have been successful. Good programmes are based on frank and scientifically accurate information about sex and HIV. They make HIV a personal and real issue, going beyond an intellectual understanding to something which young people realise can – and does – affect their lives. Good prevention programmes explain that HIV is just a virus, rather than something that marks out a good person from a bad person. But at the same time, they deal with relationships and power dynamics – the human dimensions that are so crucial to preventing the spread of the virus. They encourage open discussions about sex without moralising, letting people choose for themselves how they want to lead their sexual lives. They recognise that different people come with different experiences even if they are in the same age group and gender. Rather than worrying constantly about how people *should* behave, they start from recognition of how people *do* behave. Good programmes give people a range of options from which to choose rather than dictating just one solution or path. They do not impose on people or 'close down' what people should know; rather they involve 'opening up' and respecting people to make their own choices. This is a truly comprehensive or holistic approach and this is what works.

Unfortunately the dominant trend is moving in a different direction. HIV prevention is now becoming an intensely political arena where ideology is trampling over science. Despite clear evidence that comprehensive or holistic approaches have made a real difference, religious ideology is in the ascendance and proven methods count for little. The government of George W. Bush has more or less dismantled sex education in public schools in the US, and given a free hand to evangelical groups in the US to use HIV as a cover for proselytising in schools. This strategy is now being exported around the world. Apparently generous commitments of aid for HIV and AIDS are largely tied to the promotion of abstinence-only approaches. These approaches are proven not to work – but scientific evidence counts for little with these evangelical groups. The impact is already being felt with rising rates of HIV infection in countries such as Uganda that had previously seemed to have turned the corner.

Thankfully the abstinence-only movement is a relative newcomer and it may not be too late for many countries to reject the ideologically driven HIV prevention agenda which is imposed on them. But if they are to do this, then leadership is needed from the wider international community. The United Nations should logically play this role – but to date they have been unable to take leadership in HIV prevention because they cannot take strong political positions. The UN cannot take the side of sex workers or gay men for fear of upsetting the sensitivities of particular member states.

Indeed, the politics of aid determines who is targeted for HIV prevention and with what message. The lethal combination of evangelical groups and the American government has discredited and undermined attempts to promote condoms for HIV prevention. 'Deviant' groups such as sex workers, gay men or drug users have become invisible to many governments.

The inefficiencies of the aid system have meant that far too much money has been wasted on overly complicated models of HIV prevention which are designed far away, and without genuine reference to the people they are supposed to help. Many of the programmes are patronising, treating the developing child as a person unable to think for themselves or analyse the world. This needs to change.

Most of all, national governments across Africa, Asia and Latin America need to take the initiative themselves. Governments have the right to set their own priorities: in education, in health and in HIV prevention. But too often the international aid system undermines sovereignty and democracy. Most government spending on education and health goes on paying the salaries of teachers, doctors and nurses and very little money is left for delivering particular programmes. Donors liaise directly with ministries so most aid-funded programmes avoid parliamentary scrutiny. Aid money has rarely been spent to support the core functioning of education or health systems. Instead, all too often parallel programmes are set up which remove skilled people from government and undermine government provision of basic services.

The aid industry needs to change in many ways. It promotes short-termism at a time when long-term planning is urgently needed. It promotes parallel efforts in small projects when a coherent national response is urgently required. It is ideologically driven but pretends not to be. For all the rhetoric of putting governments in poor countries 'in the driving seat', attempts to coordinate aid through the Global Fund or the Fast Track Initiative are constantly undermined by certain donor governments, such as the American government, that insists on implementing their own bilateral programmes, dictating who should be targeted and how. This discredits aid and runs the risk of being seen as little more than a colonial legacy.

If aid is to have a role in addressing the global crises in HIV and education then donor countries have to be willing to relinquish their control over how aid money is spent. They need truly to respect the right of governments to develop their own policies and plans, promoting scrutiny of these by national parliaments and ensuring that national citizens, not donors, hold governments accountable.

Donor countries also have to move towards pledging more predictable, long-term aid, and delivering it in a coordinated way.

There are trends in this direction and the changes we propose are not inconceivable – but they will require a significant shift of power. This power shift is not dissimilar to that which is needed for successful HIV prevention in many parts of the world: the powerless need the confidence to assert their voice and the powerful need to change their ingrained attitudes and behaviours.

Beyond the aid industry there are other changes needed in the international system. The IMF needs to acknowledge the negative impact that its policies are having on internationally agreed goals in health and education. Governments in poor countries are under pressure to sacrifice desperately needed spending on education and health in the quest for macroeconomic stability. We argue that international financial institutions such as the IMF or the World Bank should offer options from which countries can choose for themselves their own path towards economic development and stability. This means respecting countries to make their own best judgments.

The resonances between the changes needed in international relations and the changes needed in human relations to achieve HIV prevention are startling. There is an echo again in the changes needed within the learning process. Successful HIV prevention depends on respecting learners, acknowledging their real experiences and enabling them to engage actively as equals.

These connections are not coincidental. They show that there is an underlying politics to the prevention of HIV that cuts through every level of analysis. As the Brazilian educator Paulo Freire observed, all education is political. There is no neutral education.

HIV prevention is becoming a defining issue of our times. As such it provides a lens to analyse the world today. It is a lens through which we can gain new perspectives on, and a new sense of urgency for, addressing the day-to-day problems experienced by marginalised groups in society. It is a lens that offers new insights on the profound injustices that still lie at the heart of many personal relationships. It is a lens through which we can see the distorting power dynamics of the international system. None of these can be addressed in isolation. Let us recognise that successful HIV prevention requires a political engagement.

Although it need not be, for many millions of people, a diagnosis of HIV is still a death sentence. This is a violation of rights on a massive scale and requires a commensurate political response. It is time for us all to recognise, as certain religious groups and governments have, that HIV prevention is one of the key political battlegrounds of our times. Access to treatment has already become a political battle in which tens of thousands of people have campaigned for cheaper AIDS drugs. Those campaigners are winning the battle against the pharmaceutical companies. The problem with HIV prevention is that, despite being highly political, at present, it is a one-sided battle. The abstinence-only movement has the money and is gaining ground in dictating what HIV prevention should be. Apart from the fact that this ideologically driven approach will not prevent HIV, we risk undermining other gains made in recent years – in terms of gender equality, human rights, social liberalism and freedom of expression.

We hope that the stories in this book have helped you to understand the politics of HIV prevention and will inspire you to unite against ideologically driven HIV prevention programmes. Alternatives are possible but it will take compassion and conviction to achieve the changes that are now long overdue.

Notes

INTRODUCTION

1. See Page of UNAIDS 2007 update: http://data.unaids.org/pub/EPISlides/2007/2007_epiupdate_en.pdf.
2. See UNAIDS updates: www.unaids.org/en/HIV_data/2007 EpiUpdate/default.asp.
3. See ibid.
4. See ibid.
5. www.who.int/hiv/topics/vct/en/index.html.
6. See ICRW report: www.icrw.org/docs/2005_report_stigma_synthesis.pdf.
7. UNAIDS, 2006, *Report on the Global AIDS Epidemic*, Geneva, 2006.
8. EFA Global Monitoring Report, UNESCO, 2007.
9. The figures in this paragraph are from the 2007 report from the Global Prevention Working Group.
10. UNAIDS, *Resource Needs for an Expanded Response to AIDS in Low- and Middle-income Countries*, Geneva, 2005.
11. See the Global HIV Prevention Working Group, 2007: www.globalhivprevention.org/pdfs/PWG-Scaling-Up-ExecSumm.pdf.

CHAPTER 1

1. UNAIDS/WHO November 2007. www.unaids.org/en/HIV_data/2007EpiUpdate/default.asp.
2. See UNAIDS updates: www.unaids.org/en/HIV_data/2007EpiUpdate/default.asp.
3. See country profiles for up-to-date prevalence estimates. www.unaids.org/en/Regions_Countries/Countries/default.asp. Accessed December 2007. These countries had prevalence rates of around 20 percent.
4. West Africa was previously thought to have a number of generalised epidemics but it now seems that HIV is still mostly confined to certain key populations and their partners.
5. An epidemic is defined as generalised once more than 1 per cent of women tested at antenatal clinics are found to have HIV.
6. 2007 UNAIDS Epidemiological Update.
7. See the 2007 UNAIDS Epidemiological Update, p.26, for update on situation in Eastern Europe.
8. For an overview on school-fee abolition in Uganda and other East African countries see: www.create-rpc.org/pdf%20documents/pathwaystoaccess10.pdf. For more general information about school-fee abolition see: http://ungei.org/infobycountry/files/HighlightsSFAIWorkshopNairobiApril2006.pdf.
9. See http://hab.hrsa.gov/publications/stigma/summary.htm.

10. Stigmatisation as experienced by a group of people living with HIV/AIDS in Dar es Salaam, Tanzania; see Riziki, J.F. and C.B. Corrigan *Int Conf AIDS*. 2002 Jul 7–12; 14: abstract no. ThPeF7971.
11. Interview with teenage member of Body and Soul, London, UK.
12. www.who.int/hiv/topics/vct/en/index.html.
13. See the ICRW report at www.icrw.org/docs/2005_report_stigma_synthesis. pdf.
14. Galletly, C.L. and S.D. Pinkerton, 2006, 'Conflicting messages: how criminal HIV disclosure laws undermine public health efforts to control the spread of HIV', *AIDS Behaviour*, June 28.
15. See www.aidsmap.com/en/docs/C92D5639-E779-44EC-B8F8-0CECCC23275A.asp.
16. McGinn, D., 'MSNBC: AIDS at 20: Anatomy of a Plague; an Oral History', Newsweek Web Exclusive and MMWR Weekly, 1981, 'Pneumocystis Pneumonia – Los Angeles', June 5, 30 (21), pp.1–3.
17. This is a quote from the AIDS history project at NIH: http://aidshistory.nih.gov/first_encounters/index.html.
18. See www.avert.org/his81_86.htm.
19. *Mail on Sunday,* 1 May 1983, cited at www.avert.org/his81_86.htm, November 2007.
20. This section on the history of AIDS is taken from avert.org: www.avert.org/his81_86.htm.
21. www.aegis.com/topics/timeline/default.asp.
22. Interview with NGO HIV policy analysts.
23. www.who.int/topics/hiv_infections/en/.
24. Quinn, T.C., J.M. Mann, J.W. Curran and P. Piot, 1986, 'AIDS in Africa: An Epidemiologic Paradigm', *Science*, 234: pp.955–63.
25. UNAIDS 2007 epidemiological update: www.unaids.org/en/HIV_data/2007EpiUpdate/default.asp.
26. See www.who.int/hiv/treatment/en/.
27. http://archives.cnn.com/2002/HEALTH/conditions/07/10/aids.costs/.
28. www.avert.org/generic.htm.
29. ww5.aegis.org/news/re/2001/RE011009.html.
30. www.who.int/hiv/mediacentre/news57/en/index.html.
31. www.who.int/hiv/treatment/en/.
32. 2007 UNAIDS epidemiological update.
33. Interview with Teo.

CHAPTER 2

1. www.unaids.org/en/Issues/Impact_HIV/default.asp.
2. Barnett, T. and A. Whiteside, 2002, *AIDS in the Twenty-First Century*. New York: Palgrave Macmillan.
3. Whiteside, A., 2000, 'The real challenges: the orphan generation and employment creation', *AIDS Anal Afr* 2000; 10(4) pp.14–15.
4. Coombe, C., *Managing the Impact of HIV/AIDS on the Education Sector*, University of Pretoria, 2000.

5. Barnett, T. and A. Whiteside, *Poverty and HIV/AIDS: Impact, Coping and Mitigation Policy*, Florence: UNICEF, 2002.

6. Whiteside, A. 'Monitoring the AIDS pandemic', *AIDS Anal Afr* 1998; 8(5) pp.4–5.

7. www.uniteforchildren.org/knowmore/knowmore_29012.htm.

8. See UNICEF estimates and reports at: www.uniteforchildren.org/.

9. See page 8 of the 2007 UNAIDS Epidemiological Update: www.unaids.org/en/HIV_data/2007EpiUpdate/default.asp.

10. See www.unaids.org/en/HIV_data/2007EpiUpdate/default.asp, p.24.

11. Despite managing to keep HIV rates under control amongst sex workers, the Thai government has been less successful in responding to HIV risks among injecting drug users, with the World Health Organisation estimating that between 30 and 50 per cent of this high-risk group is HIV-positive.

12. See UNICEF: *Children and AIDS: A Stocktaking Report*, p.9.

13. Interview with Namphung, AIDS Access. Chiang Rai, Thailand.

14. ActionAid, 2003, *Global Education Review*, London: ActionAid.

15. See UK Working Group: 'Addressing the educational needs of orphans and vulnerable children', at www.actionaid.org/assets/pdf/HIVorphans.pdf and Tania Boler, 2006, 'Facing the consequences of AIDS: orphans, cash grants and educational outcomes', PhD thesis, London School of Hygiene and Tropical Medicine, Centre for Population Studies.

16. Skinner, D., N. Tsheko, S. Mtero-Munyati, M. Segwabe, P. Chibatamoto, S. Mfecane et al. *Definition of Orphaned and Vulnerable Children*, Cape Town: HSRC, 2004.

17. UNICEF, 2005, *Children on the Brink*, New York: UNICEF.

18. See UNAIDS updates: www.unaids.org/en/HIV_data/2007EpiUpdate/default.asp.

19. Lloyd, C. and S. Desai, 1992, 'Children's living arrangements in developing countries', *Population Research and Policy Review,* 11(3), pp.193–216.

20. Foster, G., 1997, 'Africa's children and AIDS – a continent in crisis', *The Devastation of the HIV/AIDS Pandemic, AIDSlink,* 45, pp.4–5.

21. Gregson, S., H. Waddell and S. Chandiwana, 2001, 'School Education and HIV Control in Sub-Saharan Africa: From Discord to Harmony?' *Journal of International Development,* 13, pp.467–85.

22. Desmond, C. and J. Gow, 2002, 'Current and Future Impact of the HIV/AIDS Epidemic on South Africa's Children', in G. Andrea Cornia (ed.), *AIDS, Public Policy and Child Well-Being*, Florence: UNICEF, Innocenti Research Centre, 2002.

23. UNICEF, 2003, *Africa's Orphaned Generations*, New York: UNICEF.

24. ActionAid report by Boler and Carroll: Addressing the Educational Needs of Orphans and Vulnerable Children. 2004, at: www.actionaid.org/assets/pdf/HIVorphans.pdf; UNICEF, 2005, *Children on the Brink*, New York: UNICEF; and Tania Boler 'Facing the consequences of AIDS: orphans, cash grants and educational outcomes', PhD thesis, London School of Hygiene and Tropical Medicine, School of Population Studies.

25. Timæus, Ian and Tania Boler, 2007, *Father Figures: the Progress at School of Orphans in South Africa,* AIDS 2007, 21 (suppl 7): S83–S93.

26. Boler, Tania, 'Facing the consequences of AIDS: orphans, cash grants and educational outcomes'. PhD thesis, London School of Hygiene and Tropical Medicine, School of Population Studies.

27. UNESCO, EFA Global Monitoring Report, Paris 2008.

28. Ibid. http://unesdoc.unesco.org/images/0015/001548/154820e.pdf.

29. Ibid.

30. ActionAid, 2003, *Global Education Review*, London: ActionAid.

31. UNESCO, EFA Global Monitoring Report, Paris, 2008. http://unesdoc. unesco.org/images/0015/001548/154820e.pdf.

32. See the GCE report, 'A fair chance: attaining gender equality in basic education by 2005', at: www.campaignforeducation.org/resources/ Apr2003/Fair0403_EN.pdf.

33. UNESCO IIEP, 2003, *Education for Rural Development: Towards New Policy Responses*.

34. Evidence collected for the Global Education Review, ActionAid, 2003.

35. Ainsworth, M. and D. Filmer, 2002, *Poverty, AIDS, and Children's Schooling*, Washington DC: World Bank, p.41; and Case, A. and C. Ardington, 2005, 'The impact of parental death on school enrolment and achievement: longitudinal evidence from South Africa', World Bank, Working Paper 43.

36. UNESCO, EFA Global Monitoring Report, Paris, 2008. http://unesdoc. unesco.org/images/0015/001548/154820e.pdf.

37. UNAIDS, 2006, Report on the Global AIDS Epidemic, Geneva, 2006.

38. See GCE, 2006, Right to Education during Displacement: A Resource for Organizations Working with Refugees and Internally Displaced Persons. www.campaignforeducation.org/resources/Aug2006/Right%20to%20Ed ucation%20During%20Displacement.pdf.

39. See UNHCR reports, for example: www.fmreview.org/FMRpdfs/FMR19/ FMR1909.pdf.

40. EFA, GMR 2007.

41. Interviews with NGOs in Tamil Nadu, India.

42. Global Education Review, ActionAid, 2003.

43. See *Education Action*, 21, 2007, ActionAid or visit www.mvfindia.org.

44. Tomasevski, K., 2006, *The State of the Right to Education Worldwide. Free or Fee: 2006 Global Report*, Copenhagen.

45. See the GCE report, 2006: *In the Public Interest: Health, Education, and Water and Sanitation for All.*

46. See the GCE report, 'A fair chance: Attaining gender equality in basic education by 2005', at: www.campaignforeducation.org/resources/ Apr2003/Fair0403_EN.pdf.

47. Global Education Review. London: ActionAid, 2003.

48. See www.globalaidsalliance.org.

49. See www.ungei.org, for details of the School Fee Abolition Initiative.

50. ActionAid report by Boler and Carroll: Addressing the Educational Needs of Orphans and Vulnerable Children, 2004: www.actionaid.org/assets/ pdf/HIVorphans.pdf.

51. Case, A. and C. Ardington, 2005, 'The impact of parental death on school enrolment and achievement: longitudinal evidence from South Africa', World Bank, Working Paper 43.

52. Boler, T., 2006, 'Facing the consequences of AIDS: orphans, cash grants and educational outcomes', PhD thesis, London School of Hygiene and Tropical Medicine, School of Population Studies.
53. See Chapter 4 of the study 'Violence against Children', at: www. violencestudy.org/IMG/pdf/4._World_Report_on_Violence_against_ Children.pdf.

CHAPTER 3

1. UNAIDS, 2006, Report on the Global AIDS Epidemic, Geneva.
2. See the 2007 UNAIDS Report on the Global AIDS Epidemic, p.8.
3. See the UNAIDS report: Women and AIDS: Confronting the Crisis: http:// genderandaids.org/downloads/conference/308_filename_women_aids1. pdf.
4. Hargreaves, J. and T. Boler, 2006, *Girl Power: The Impact of Girls' Education on HIV and Sexual Behaviour,* ActionAid International.
5. Luke, N., 2003, 'Age and economic asymmetries in the sexual relationships of adolescent girls in sub-Saharan Africa', *Studies in Family Planning,* 34(2) pp.67–86, and Varga, C.A., 1997, 'Sexual decision-making and negotiation in the midst of AIDS: youth in KwaZulu-Natal, South Africa', *Health Transition Review* (supplement) 7, pp.45–67.
6. Gilbert, L. and L. Walker, 2002, 'Treading the path of least resistance: HIV/AIDS and social inequalities – a South African case study', *Social Science and Medicine,* 54(7), pp.1093–100.
7. Kaufman, C. and S.E. Stavrou, '"Bus fare, please": The economics of sex and gifts among adolescents in urban South Africa', New York: Population Council, 2002.
8. MacPhail, C. and C. Campbell, 2001, '"I think condoms are good but, aaai, I hate those things": condom use among adolescents and young people in a Southern African township', *Social Science and Medicine,* 52, pp.1613–27.
9. Wellesley Centers for Research on Women, 2003, 'Unsafe schools: a literature review of school-related gender-based violence in developing countries', Washington DC: USAID.
10. This section is an extract from the ActionAid report: Hargreaves, J. and T. Boler, 2006, *Girl Power: The Impact of Girls' Education on HIV and Sexual Behaviour,* ActionAid International.
11. See Chapter 4 of the study 'Violence against Children': www.violencestudy. org/IMG/pdf/4._World_Report_on_Violence_against_Children.pdf.
12. *Making the Grade: a Model Policy,* OSISA and ActionAid 2006.
13. Ibid.
14. See *Education Action,* Issue 22, January 2008.
15. Boler, T., R. Adoss, A. Ibrahim and M. Shaw, 2003, *The Sound of Silence: Difficulties in Communicating on HIV/AIDS in Schools,* London: ActionAid International, 2003.
16. See *Contradicting Commitments: How the Achievement of EFA is Undermined by the IMF,* ActionAid 2005.
17. See *Confronting the Contradictions: The IMF, Wage Bill Caps and the Case for Teachers,* ActionAid 2007.

18. Adrian Verspoor, presenting at the Association for Development of Education in Africa conference in Gabon in 2006: 'class size up to 60 does not affect student performance'. 'Long pre-service programs show little evidence of improved learning but do imply higher salary cost'. 'Non-civil service contract teacher programmes may be successfully introduced without compromising education quality'.

19. See www.ei-ie.org.

20. See, for example, *From Schooling Access to Learning Outcomes: An Unfinished Agenda: An Evaluation of World Bank Support to Primary Education*, IEG, World Bank 2006. Particularly revealing are the independent country evaluations in Mali, Pakistan and Uganda that fed into this wider evaluation – though the full findings of these were not well reflected in the World Bank's own final evaluation.

21. This and subsequent quotes are from interviews with the authors in 2005.

22. EFA Global Monitoring Report 2007.

23. Ibid.

24. ActionAid, Global Education Review 2003.

25. Examples from Ghana, Niger and India taken from *From Schooling Access to Learning Outcomes: An Unfinished Agenda: An Evaluation of World Bank Support to Primary Education*, IEG, World Bank 2006.

26. ActionAid, Global Education Review 2003.

27. See the EFA Global Monitoring Report 2005 on Quality Education.

28. From *From Schooling Access to Learning Outcomes: An Unfinished Agenda: An Evaluation of World Bank Support to Primary Education*, IEG, World Bank 2006, ch4.

CHAPTER 4

1. Global HIV Prevention Working Group, 2007, 'Bringing HIV Prevention to Scale: An urgent global priority', at: www.globalhivprevention.org/pdfs/PWG-HIV_prevention_report_FINAL.pdf.

2. Ibid.

3. See the CDC's history of the response at: www.cdc.gov/mmwR/preview/mmwrhtml/mm5521a4.htm.

4. Cited on p.14 of Global HIV Prevention Working Group paper, 2007.

5. UNAIDS officials in personal communication.

6. www.who.int/hiv/topics/malecircumcision/en/.

7. Studies such as those by Mema Kwa Vijana show a positive impact on knowledge and attitudes but no impact on biological outcomes such as STI rates or HIV rates. For Mema Kwa Vijana see: www.amref.org/docs/Impact%20Evaluation%20MEMA%20kwa%20Vijana.pdf.

8. Pregnancy is a sign that unprotected sex has been taking place.

9. See: www.amref.org/docs/Impact%20Evaluation%20MEMA%20kwa%20Vijana.pdf.

10. This list is taken from the UK Working Group paper on The Abstinence Debate: Condoms, Pepfar and Ideology, 2007: www.aidsportal.org/repos/AbstinenceDebateEducationReport07.pdf.

11. See the analysis by Boler and Aggleton, 2005: www.actionaid.org/assets/ pdf/life_skills_new_small_version.pdf.
12. This section on structuralist and rational approaches is based on an extract from Boler and Aggleton, 2005, ActionAid: www.actionaid.org/ assets/pdf/life_skills_new_small_version.pdf.
13. See the UNAIDS Ghana country profile: www.unaids.org/en/ CountryResponses/Countries/ghana.asp.
14. See p.28 of the GCE report: Boler, T. and A. Jellema, 'Deadly Inertia: a cross-country study of educational responses to HIV/AIDS', Johannesburg: Global Campaign for Education, 2005.
15. Interview with Theatre for a Change; and Boler, T. and A. Jellema 'Deadly Inertia: a cross-country study of educational responses to HIV/AIDS', Johannesburg: Global Campaign for Education, 2005.
16. See www.tfacafrica.com.
17. Participatory learning methodologies are approaches that involve both the learner and the educator. Rather than passive learning it is more active and will include participation from the learner.
18. This section on Theatre for a Change is drawn from a chapter written by one of the authors (Tania Boler) and Lucy Stackpool-Moore, based on an interview with Theatre for Change by Tania Boler for the book *Combating Gender Violence in and around Schools*, edited by Fiona Leach and Claudia Mitchell, Oakham: Trentham Books.
19. For a detailed critique of this approach to life skills, which includes accelerated programmes to teach 'assertiveness', see Chapter 8.
20. Aggleton, P., E. Chase and K. Rivers, 'HIV/AIDS prevention and care among especially vulnerable young people: a framework for action', London: Thomas Coram Research Institute, 2004.
21. See *Sound of Silence*, 2003 Boler, T. et al., at ActionAid: www.actionaid. org/docs/hivsoundofsilence.pdf.
22. Paris Declaration by Heads of State. GIPA Principles.
23. Interviews with UN PLUS members.
24. Interview with MANASCO in Mozambique.
25. See the EFA Global Monitoring Report: http://unesdoc.unesco.org/ images/0015/001548/154820e.pdf.
26. Hargreaves, J. and J. Glynn, 2002, 'Educational attainment and HIV-1 infection in developing countries: a systematic review', *Tropical Medicine and International Health* 7(6) pp.489–98.
27. There is more information on both Soul City and Soul Buddyz at www. soulcity.org.za.
28. UNAIDS, 2003, National Response Brief. South Africa: UNAIDS.
29. South Africa does not have the highest prevalence rates but given the size of her population, has the largest actual number. See p.16 of UNAIDS Epidemiological update 2007: www.unaids.org/en/HIV_data/ 2007EpiUpdate/default.asp.
30. CIA: *World Factbook, 2003.*
31. For full history of South Africa's response see: www.avert.org/aidssoutha-frica.htm.
32. See Mark Gevisser, *Thabo Mbeki: The Dream Deferred*, Exclusive Books, 2007.

33. See: www.aegis.com/news/woza/2000/IC000906.html.
34. http://news.bbc.co.uk/1/hi/world/africa/5319680.stm.
35. http://news.bbc.co.uk/1/hi/world/africa/5265432.stm.
36. www.unaids.org/en/HIV_data/2007EpiUpdate/default.asp.
37. Haiti and Zambia for women only. www.unaids.org/en/HIV_data/ 2007EpiUpdate/default.asp.

CHAPTER 5

1. UNAIDS, 2006, Report on the Global AIDS Epidemic, Geneva, 2006.
2. From interview with AIDS Access, Chiang Raid, Thailand.
3. See the EFA Global Monitoring Report 2005: The Quality Imperative.
4. See, for example www.unicef.org/lifeskills/index_7260.html for details of their framework for rights-based, child-friendly educational systems and schools.
5. Quote from the Society for Quality Education, see www. societyforqualityeducation.org/parents/.
6. www.societyforqualityeducation.org/.
7. www.societyforqualityeducation.org/parents/.
8. See UNESCO, 2005, *Strengthening Inclusive Education by Applying a Rights-based Approach to Education Programming* at: www.unescobkk.org/ fileadmin/user_upload/appeal/IE/Publications_and_reports/OS_ISEC_ 2005_Paper.pdf.
9. EFA Global Monitoring Report 2005: The Quality Imperative.
10. See www.fawe.org.
11. Presentation by Rose from FAWE in Abuja, Nigeria, December 2007.
12. See UNESCO 2008 report: 'School-centred HIV and AIDS care and support in Southern Africa'.
13. Interview with Soul Buddyz, South Africa.
14. Along with Spain, Italy and France. See p.24 of UNAIDS 2007 Epidemiological Update.
15. EuroHIV, 2007 cited in UNAIDS 2007 Epidemiological Update p.34.
16. See www.bodyandsoulcharity.org.
17. From an interview with Amos at Kindlimuka, Mozambique.
18. Passed by Parliament in February 2002.

CHAPTER 6

1. www.avert.org/aids-brazil.htm.
2. Personal communication with John Cleland.
3. Interview with Gabriella.
4. Based on interviews with the Brazilian Department of Health in Rio de Janeiro.
5. Wu Chou, 1975, *Report from Tungting – A People's Commune on Taihu Lake*, Beijing Foreign Languages Press.
6. This entire section is based on interviews with Gabriella and Celia.
7. Freire, P., 1998, *Pedagogy of the Heart*, Continuum International Publishing Group, p.80.
8. Freire, *Pedagogy of the Heart*.

9. See www.reflect-action.org. Reflect was inspired by Paulo Freire and was developed in Uganda, Bangladesh and El Salvador in parallel pilot projects. It is now used by over 500 organisations in 70 countries, reaching millions of adult learners. STAR evolved from Reflect and was given a new name in 2005. For more information on STAR, contact ActionAid International.

10. www.un.org/Overview/rights.html.

11. Katarina passed away in 2006. One of her most enduring legacies was the right-to-education project – see www.right-to-education.org. As the former UN Special Rapporteur on the Right to Education she was formidable in challenging both the World Bank and governments (from the US to China) about their violation of education rights.

12. This quote is from a collection of essays entitled *Ethics and Law in the Study of AIDS* (published in 1992 by the Panamerican Health Organization).

13. These are taken from Education Rights Project in South Africa: 'HIV and AIDS: The Rights of Learners and Educators'.

14. In Kenya, Angelo D'Agostino won a landmark lawsuit against the Kenyan public school system for turning away HIV-positive children, and two cases were also won in Kerala, India.

15. www.unaids.org/en/HIV_data/2007EpiUpdate/default.asp.

16. This quote is from an extract from a *Times Online* article: www.timesonline. co.uk/tol/news/world/asia/article1907367.ece.

17. This quote is taken from a BBC article: http://news.bbc.co.uk/1/hi/world/ south_asia/6727465.stm.

18. For full story see the BBC article: http://news.bbc.co.uk/1/hi/world/ south_asia/6727465.stm.

19. See: http://fe18.news.sp1.yahoo.com/s/afp/20070625/hl_afp/healthin diaaids.

20. Tomasevski, K., 2005, 'Human Rights and Poverty Reduction: Why a Human Rights Approach to HIV/AIDS Makes all the Difference'. www. odi.org.uk/rights/Meeting%20Series/HIVAIDS_HRBA.pdf.

21. This story is taken from www.allafrica.com. For specific story visit: http:// allafrica.com/stories/200706190435.html.

CHAPTER 7

1. Abma, J.C. et al., 'Teenagers in the United States: sexual activity, contraceptive use, and childbearing, 2002', *Vital and Health Statistics*, 2004, Series 23, No. 24. DC figures quoted in UNAIDS 2007 Epidemiological Update page 33.

2. Ibid.

3. Ibid.

4. Weinstock, H., et al., 'Sexually transmitted diseases among American youth: incidence and prevalence estimates, 2000', *Perspectives on Sexual and Reproductive Health*, 2004, 36(1) pp.6–10; Darroch, J.E., J.J. Frost and S. Singh, 2001, 'Teenage sexual and reproductive behavior in developed countries: can more progress be made?', *Occasional Report*, New York: The Alan Guttmacher Institute, No. 3.

5. Singh, S. and J.E. Darroch, 1998, 'Adolescent pregnancy and childbearing: levels and trends in developed countries', *Family Planning Perspectives,* 32(1) pp.14–23.

6. www.guttmacher.org/pubs/fb_ATSRH.html#ref1.

7. www.guttmacher.org/pubs/tgr/05/1/gr050107.html.

8. Bleakley, A., et al., 2006, 'Public opinion on sex education in US schools', *Archives of Pediatrics and Adolescent Medicine,* 160(11) pp.1151–6.

9. Darroch, J.E., et al., 2000, 'Changing emphases in sexuality education in US public secondary schools, 1988–1999', *Family Planning Perspectives,* 32(5) pp.204–11 and 265.

10. www.advocatesforyouth.org/publications/factsheet/fshistoryabonly. htm.

11. States are required to spend $3 for every $4 of federal funding. See: www. advocatesforyouth.org/publications/factsheet/fshistoryabonly.htm.

12. www.advocatesforyouth.org/publications/factsheet/fsmythsfacts.htm.

13. www.guttmacher.org/pubs/fb_sexEd2006.html#25.

14. Two thirds of districts decide their own policy and in the remainder, schools decide themselves. See: www.guttmacher.org/pubs/fb_sexEd2006. html#19a.

15. From interview with Nancy Kendall about sex education in Florida.

16. Darroch, J.E., et al., 2000, 'Changing emphases in sexuality education in US public secondary schools, 1988–1999', *Family Planning Perspectives,* 32(5) pp.204–11 and 265.

17. www.guttmacher.org/pubs/fb_sexEd2006.html#24.

18. Florida received $2.2 million in federal Title V funding for federal fiscal year and $3.5 million in state funds to support abstinence-only programmes in 2003, *SIECUS State Profiles: A Portrait of Sexuality Education and Abstinence-only-until-marriage Programs in the United States, Fiscal Year 2003 Edition.* New York, 2004.

19. Florida State University School of Social Work. *Florida DOH Abstinence Education Providers Pretest/Posttest Analysis.* Tallahassee, FL: Florida State University and Florida Department of Health, 2002–03.

20. Nancy Kendall in interview.

21. www.cdc.gov/std/hpv/STDFact-HPV-vaccine.htm.

22. Classroom observation in Pensacola.

23. Santelli, J.S., et al., 2007, 'Explaining recent declines in adolescent pregnancy in the United States: the contribution of abstinence and improved contraceptive use', *American Journal of Public Health,* 2007, 97(1) pp.1–7.

24. Kirby, D., 2001, *Emerging Answers: Research Findings on Programs to Reduce Teen Pregnancy,* Washington, DC: National Campaign to Prevent Teen Pregnancy, 2001.

25. Ibid.

26. Underhill, K., P. Montgomery, D. Operario, 2007, 'Sexual-abstinence-only programmes to prevent HIV infection in high income countries: systematic review', *British Medical Journal,* July, p.335.

27. Interviews with groups in Florida.

28. www.pepfar.gov/press/81352.htm.

29. See Boler and Ingham, 2007: www.actionaid.org/assets/pdf%5Caa_ abstinence_reportPRINT.pdf.
30. See Bernstein, R.S., D.C. Sokal, S.T. Seitz, B. Auvert, W. Naamara, and J. Stover, 2004, 'Partner reduction is crucial for balanced "ABC" approach to HIV prevention', *British Medical Journal* April, 328, pp.891–3; Also at: www.bmj.com/cgi/content/full/328/7444/891.
31. The 2004 '5-year strategy of the President's Emergency Plan for AIDS Relief' states on page 11 'Uganda's success has identified the "ABC" model (Abstinence, Be faithful, and, as appropriate, correctly and consistently use Condoms) as an effective HIV/AIDS prevention tool. We will promote the proper application of the ABC approach, through population-specific interventions that emphasize abstinence for youth, including the delay of sexual debut and abstinence until marriage; HIV/AIDS testing and fidelity in marriage and monogamous relationships; and correct and consistent use of condoms for those who practice high-risk behaviours.' Also see the five-year PEPFAR strategy: www.state.gov/documents/organization/29831. pdf.
32. Page 27 of the five-year PEPFAR strategy: www.state.gov/documents/ organization/29831.pdf.
33. Ibid.
34. Cited in November 2007 at: www.globalhealth.org/view_top. php3?id=227.
35. For more in-depth discussion of PIASCY and how it was affected by PEPFAR, see the Human Rights Watch report on: http://hrw.org/english/ docs/2006/02/01/uganda12591_txt.htm.
36. USAID funded a technical adviser in the Ministry of Education to oversee the process; Beatrice Were in interview.
37. Analysis of new PIASCY curriculum is based on interviews with Beatrice Were.
38. Human Rights Watch, 2005, 'The Less They Know, the Better. Abstinence-Only HIV/AIDS Programs in Uganda', Vol. 17, No. 4(A). New York: Human Rights Watch, 2005.
39. www.unaids.org/en/HIV_data/2007EpiUpdate/default.asp.
40. See p.18: www.unaids.org/en/HIV_data/2007EpiUpdate/default.asp.
41. http://hrw.org/reports/2005/uganda0305/1.htm.

CHAPTER 8

1. www.populationaction.org/Publications/Fact_Sheets/FS25/Summary. shtml.
2. www.peopleandplanet.net/doc.php?id=2598.
3. www.actupny.org/reports/globalgagrule.html.
4. www.actupny.org/reports/globalgagrule.html.
5. For the full story: http://thinkprogress.org/2007/04/28/ross-white-house-madam/.
6. www.nswp.org/ – a response to a UNAIDS guidance note.
7. www.sexworkeurope.org/site/images/PDFs/the%20curious%20sex%20 worker.pdf.

8. www.fco.gov.uk/servlet/Front?pagename=OpenMarket/Xcelerate/Show
   Page&c=Page&cid=1007029391647&a=KArticle&aid=1152525661291
   and www.actwin.com/eatonohio/gay/sodomy.html.
9. www.fco.gov.uk/servlet/Front?pagename=OpenMarket/Xcelerate/Show
   Page&c=Page&cid=1007029391647&a=KArticle&aid=1152525661291.
10. See the chapter by Hoffmann, Boler and Dick in *Preventing HIV/AIDS
    among Young People. A Systematic Review of the Evidence in Developing
    Countries*. 2006 WHO Technical Report Series, at: http://whqlibdoc.who.
    int/trs/WHO_TRS_938_eng.pdf.
11. DesJarlais, 2005. Cited on page 14 of Global HIV Prevention Working
    Group *Bringing HIV Prevention to Scale: An Urgent Global Priority*, at: www.
    globalhivprevention.org/pdfs/PWG-HIV_prevention_report_FINAL.
    pdf.
12. Ibid p.2.
13. Milio, N., 2006, 'The poverty of public health in a dominant power',
    Journal of Epidemiology and Community Health, 60: pp.2–3; James, G., 1965,
    'Poverty and public health – new outlooks. I. Poverty as an obstacle to
    health progress in our cities', *American Journal of Public Health*, November,
    55(11) pp. 1757–71 and also see: www.pressureworks.org/focus/hiv/what/
    poverty.html.
14. See page 17 of the UNFPA 2005 report, 'Donor Support for Contraceptives
    and Condoms for STI/HIV Prevention', 2005.
15. Ibid. p.20.
16. See page 2 of Global HIV Prevention Working Group, 2007. *Bringing HIV
    Prevention to Scale: An Urgent Global Priority*. www.globalhivprevention.
    org/pdfs/PWG-HIV_prevention_report_FINAL.pdf.
17. www.globalgagrule.org/.
18. www.globalgagrule.org/execsum.htm.
19. www.globalpolicy.org/finance/info/agencies/2003/0122condom.htm.
20. See page 13 of the UNFPA 2005 report 'Donor Support for Contraceptives
    and Condoms for STI/HIV Prevention', 2005. www.unfpa.org/upload/
    lib_pub_file/681_filename_dsr_2005.pdf.
21. www.unfpa.org/supplies/facts.htm.
22. www.guardian.co.uk/aids/story/0,7369,1423995,00.html.
23. See page 17 of the UNFPA 2005 report 'Donor Support for Contraceptives
    and Condoms for STI/HIV Prevention', 2005.
24. See the *New York Times* article 'US Blamed for Condom Shortage in
    Fighting AIDS in Uganda', by Lawrence K. Altman. Published: August
    30, 2005.
25. Museveni's opening speech at International AIDS Conference in Bangkok,
    2004.
26. http://query.nytimes.com/gst/fullpage.html?sec=health&res=9E02E3D
    C1631F933A0575BC0A9639C8B63&fta=y.
27. See page 2 of Global HIV Prevention Working Group, 2007: www.global-
    hivprevention.org/pdfs/PWG-Scaling-Up-ExecSumm.pdf.
28. Boler, T. and A. Jellema, 2005, *Deadly Inertia: a Cross-country Study of
    Educational Responses to HIV/AIDS*, Johannesburg: Global Campaign for
    Education.

29. This section on life skills is based on the ActionAid report: Boler, T. and P. Aggleton, 2005, *Life Skills Education for HIV Prevention: a Critical Analysis*, London: Save the Children and ActionAid International.
30. Article 53 of the UNGASS declaration 2005.
31. Boler, T. and P. Aggleton, 2005, *Life Skills Education for HIV Prevention: a Critical Analysis*, London: Save the Children and ActionAid International.
32. The following section on 'deadly inertia' is based upon: Boler, T. and A. Jellema, 2005, *Deadly Inertia: a Cross-country Study of Educational Responses to HIV/AIDS*, Johannesburg: Global Campaign for Education.
33. Ibid.
34. http://news.bbc.co.uk/1/hi/world/africa/5265432.stm.
35. Schneider, Helen and Didier Fassin, 2002, 'Denial and defiance: a socio-political analysis of AIDS in South Africa', *AIDS Supplement* 16 (Supplement 4): S45–S51. Retrieved on 23 November 2006.
36. Streek, B. and D. Forrest, 2001, 'Mbeki in bizarre Aids outburst', *Mail and Guardian,* 26 October 2001.
37. See the article in the May 2003 edition of the *New Yorker* magazine by Samantha Power entitled 'The Aids Rebel' at www.pbs.org/pov/pov2003/stateofdenial/special_rebel2.html.
38. Schneider, Helen and Didier Fassin, 2002, 'Denial and defiance: a socio-political analysis of AIDS in South Africa', *AIDS Supplement* 16 (Supplement 4): S45–S51.
39. Cited in the *New Yorker* May 2003: www.pbs.org/pov/pov2003/stateofdenial/special_rebel2.html.
40. This section is based on *Thabo Mbeki: A Dream Deferred* by Mark Gevisser, 2007.
41. For an analysis of Thabo Mbeki's role in AIDS see Gevisser, *Thabo Mbeki: A Dream Deferred*.

CHAPTER 9

1. UNAIDS, 2005, *Resource Needs for an Expanded Response to AIDS in Low- and Middle-income Countries*, Geneva.
2. ActionAid, 2005, *Real Aid. An Agenda for Making Aid Work*, at www.actionaid.org.uk/100113/real_aid_1.html.
3. Ibid.
4. EFA GMR 2007.
5. See the policy brief, *Untying Aid to the Least Developed Countries*, OECD Observer 2001.
6. Kaiser Daily Report, 2004, 'US Government Accounting Office Report to International AIDS Conference'. 1 November.
7. For example, 25 of the 34 largest recipients of the UK TA contracts listed on the DfID website are British. The other nine recipients are mostly American and Canadian, and none is from a developing country. See ActionAid, 2005, *Real Aid. An Agenda for Making Aid Work*, at www.actionaid.org.uk/100113/real_aid_1.html.
8. World Bank, 2000, *Can Africa Claim the 21st Century?* New York: Oxford University Press.

9. Siddiqui, F., C. Strickler and P. Vinde, 2004, *Capacity Building Practices of Cambodia's Development Partners: Results of a Survey.*

10. 'Research on Technical Assistance to the Education Sector in Ghana', report by Daniel K.B. Inkoom for ActionAid, April 2006.

11. DAC 2003, cited in ActionAid, 2005, *Real Aid. An Agenda for Making Aid Work*, at www.actionaid.org.uk/100113/real_aid_1.html.

12. See Actionaid, 2003: Sound of Silence, at: www.ibe.unesco.org/AIDS/doc/ HIV%20AIDS%20187.pdf.

13. www.populationaction.org/Publications/Fact_Sheets/FS25/Summary. shtml.

14. Interview with a Zambian NGO, 2007.

15. Oxfam International, 2004, *Paying the Price. Why Rich Countries Must Invest Now in a War on Poverty.*

16. See ActionAid 2007: *Confronting the Contradictions: The IMF, Wage Bill Caps and the Case for Teachers*, www.actionaid.org/assets/pdf/AAConf_Contra-dictions_Final2.pdf.

17. Government of Uganda Poverty Eradication Action Plan 2004/05–2008, 2004.

18. Foster, M. and A. Keith, *The Case for Increased Aid*, 2003 Final Report to the Department for International Development.

19. See www.oecd.org or follow the link: www.oecd.org/document/18/ 0,2340,en_2649_3236398_35401554_1_1_1_1,00.html.

20. OECD is the Organisation for Economic Cooperation and Development.

21. www.fasttrackinitiative.org.

22. These statistics are based on the GCE 2008 School Report.

23. Global Fund to Fight AIDS, TB and Malaria. FAQ: Available at: www. globalfundatm.org/faq_proposal.html.

24. See ActionAid: 'The Best Chance We Have', at www.actionaid.org.uk/_ content/documents/thebestchance_3132004_115137.pdf.

25. Confidential interview with a UNAIDS employee.

26. www.globalaidsalliance.org/issues/fund_the_fight/.

27. See the US contribution: www.theglobalfund.org/en/funds_raised/ pledges/.

28. $10 billion is for PEPFAR target countries, $4 billion for other countries and $1 billion for GFATM. www.pepfar.gov/about/c19380.htm.

29. See the Global HIV Prevention Working Group, 2007: www.globalhiv prevention.org/pdfs/PWG-Scaling-Up-ExecSumm.pdf.

30. Ibid., p.14.

31. See the press statement by UNESCO: www.un.org/apps/news/story.asp? NewsID=20147&Cr=educat&Cr1.

32. WHO World Health Report, cited at: www.cbsnews.com/ stories/2006/04/07/health/main1481058.shtml.

33. See ActionAid 2005: *Confronting the Contradictions*. www.actionaid.org/ assets/pdf/contradicting_commitments4.pdf.

34. See ActionAid 2005, *Changing Course*, at www.actionaidusa.org/pdf/Cha nging%20Course%20Report.pdf.

35. See ActionAid, *Confronting the Contradictions*.

36. Ibid.

37. www.actionaid.org/main.aspx?PageID=112.

38. Personal communication with Kenyan Teachers' Commission.
39. ActionAid, 2007, *Confronting the Contradictions: The IMF, wage bill caps and the case for teachers*, London, ActionAid International.
40. As reported in *The Lancet* 2007; 370 pp.1749–50 DOI:10.1016/S0140–6736(07)61734–6.
41. 'Does the IMF constrain spending in health in poor countries? Evidence and an agenda for action', Center for Global Development, USA, June 2007.
42. This is quoted in ActionAid's 'Blocking Progress Report', at: www.afrol.com/articles/14274.
43. Rowden, R., 2004, *Blocking Progress: How the Fight against HIV/AIDS is being Undermined by the World Bank and the International Monetary Fund*, Washington DC: ActionAid International.
44. This section is based on Rowden, *Blocking Progress*.
45. ActionAid, 2005, *Changing Course: Alternative Policies to Achieve the Millennium Development Goals and Fight HIV/AIDS,* Washington DC: ActionAid International USA.
46. Independent Evaluation Office, *An Evaluation of the IMF and Aid to Sub-Saharan Africa.* 12 March 2007, also at: www.ieo-imf.org/eval/complete/pdf/03122007/report.pdf.
47. ActionAid, 2007, *Confronting the Contradictions.*
48. ActionAid, 2005, *Changing Course.*
49. See an interview with Andy Berg on the macroeconomics of managing increased aid inflows: www.imf.org/External/NP/EXR/cs/eng/2006/022406.htm.
50. ActionAid, 2005, *Changing Course.*
51. In 2007 the IMF published two papers discussing the role: 'Aid Inflows: The Role of the Fund and Operational Issues for Program Design of the IMF in relation to scaled up aid and aid inflows' (www.imf.org/external/np/pp/2007/eng/061407.pdf) and 'Fiscal Response to Scaled Up Aid' (www.imf.org/external/np/pp/2007/eng/060507.pdf). The IMF Board discussed these papers and made some commitments to adjust its working practices, which were broadcast in a Public Information Notice No. 07/83, IMF Executive Board Discusses Operational Implications of Aid Inflows (www.imf.org/external/np/sec/pn/2007/pn0783.htm).

CHAPTER 10

1. UNAIDS, 2007, AIDS epidemiological update. Geneva: UNAIDS.
2. Ibid.

Contact Organisations
for Further Information

AIDS Access Foundation
Chiang Rai
Thailand
Tel: +661 910 4884
www.aidsaccess.com

ActionAid International
PostNet suite #248
Private bag X31
Saxonwold 2132
Johannesburg
South Africa
Tel: +27 11 731 4500
Fax: +27 11 880 8082
mail.jhb@actionaid.org
www.actionaid.org

Body and Soul
99–119 Rosebery Avenue
London EC1R 4RE
UK
Tel: +44 2079236880
www.bodyandsoulcharity.org

FAWE
FAWE House, Chania Avenue Off
Wood Avenue, Kilimani, Nairobi
Mailing address:
PO Box 21394 00505 Ngong Road
Nairobi, Kenya
Tel: +254 20 3873131, 3873351,
3873359
www.fawe.org

Global AIDS Alliance
1413 K Street NW, 4th Floor
Washington, DC 20005
USA
Phone: +1 202 789 0432
Fax: +1 202 789 0715
www.globalaidsalliance.org

GCE (Global Campaign for
Education)
PO Box 521733
Saxonwold 2132
South Africa
2711 447 4111
www.campaignforeducation.org

Kindlimuka
Resistencia Avenue no. 630,
Maputo, Mozambique
Tel: +258 1 422651
Fax: +258 1 422651
kindlimuka@mail.tropical.co.mz

MV Foundation
201, Narayan Apartments,
West Marredpally,
Secunderabad – 500026, AP India.
Tel: +91 (40) 2780 1320
Fax: +91 (40) 2780 8808
mvfindia@gmail.com
www.mvfindia.in

Oxfam
Suite 20, 266 Banbury Road,
Oxford, OX2 7DL, UK
Tel: +44 1865 339 100
Fax: +44 1865 339 101
information@oxfaminternational.org
www.oxfam.org

PIM
Health in Prostitution Project,
PIM-ISER, Rua Senador Correa 48,
Laranjeiras, 22231-180
Rio de Janeiro, RJ, Brazil
Tel: +55 21 265 5747
pim.trp@terra.com.br

Population Action International
1300 19th Street, NW Suite 200
Washington, DC 20036-1624
USA
Tel: +1 (202) 557 3400
Fax: +1 (202) 728 4177
www.populationaction.org

Rede Brasileira de Prostitutas
(Brazilian Network of Sex Workers)
rede@redeprostitutas.org.br
www.redeprostitutas.org.br

Reflect
pamoja@infocom.co.ug
www.reflect-action.org

Soul Buddyz
Soul City Institute for Health and
Development Communication
PO Box 1290
Houghton 2041
South Africa
Tel: +27 (011) 341 0360
Fax: +27 (011) 341 0370
soulcity@soulcity.org.za
www.soulcity.org.za

TAC
3rd Floor, Westminster House,
122 Longmarket Street,
Cape Town 8001
Tel: +27 021 422 1700
www.tac.org.za

TASO
Old Mulago Complex
PO Box 10443, Kampala
Tel: +256 41 532580/1
Fax: +256 41 541288
mail@tasouganda.org
www.tasouganda.org

Theatre for a Change
F 645/3 South La Estate,
2nd Otswe Street,
Accra
Ghana
mob: +233 244 658284
www.theatreforachange.com

The Work of
act:onaid

We are an international anti-poverty agency which takes sides with poor people to end poverty and injustice together. Formed in 1972, for over 35 years we have been growing and expanding to where we are today – helping over 13 million of the world's poorest and most disadvantaged people in over 40 countries worldwide.

In December 2003, we established a new head office in Johannesburg, South Africa, and began the process of making all our country programmes equal partners with an equal say on how we operate.

We work with local partners to fight poverty and injustice worldwide, helping the poorest and most vulnerable people to fight for and gain their rights to food, shelter, work, education, healthcare and a voice in the decisions that affect their lives.

Our **partners** range from small community support groups to national alliances and international networks seeking education for all, trade justice and action against HIV and AIDS. Our work with these national and international campaign networks highlights the issues that affect poor people and influences the way governments and international institutions think.

Education work is part of the DNA of ActionAid and we are now widely recognised as a leading international organisation working in the sector. We play a key role in facilitating national education campaigns and co-founded the Global Campaign for Education in 1999. We jointly coordinate the Commonwealth Education Fund and since 2006 we have forged a strategic relationship with teacher unions. We have been awarded the UN International Literacy Prize for our work in conceiving, piloting and disseminating the Reflect approach to adult learning (now used by over 500 organisations in 70 countries). For us, education is a fundamental human right, the responsibility of the state and a core element of any development policy committed to social justice.

ActionAid has been working on **HIV and AIDS** since 1987, giving practical support to people living with the disease in 23 countries, as well as campaigning and lobbying rich governments and international institutions to make access to drugs, care and treatment fair and unbiased. We are working with the governments of Ethiopia, Rwanda, Burundi and Ghana to establish National AIDS Commissions and community support groups that act as lifelines in hard-hit regions. We have also played lead role in developing participatory methodologies in response to HIV and AIDS, such as STAR (Societies Tackling AIDS through Rights).

For further details of our work and to download our publications on education and HIV see: www.actionaid.org.

Index

Compiled by Sue Carlton